Caltech's Architectural Heritage

FROM SPANISH TILE TO MODERN STONE

Caltech's Architectural Heritage

FROM SPANISH TILE TO MODERN STONE

Romy Wyllie

Balcony Press   Los Angeles

To Tom and Doris

For making this book possible.
It is their legacy to Caltech.

First Printing

Published in the United States of America
Design by SchoeneHauser Design
Imaging and production by Navigator Press,
Pasadena, California
Printed in Hong Kong
No part of this book may be reproduced in any manner without
written permission except in the case of brief quotations embodied
in critical articles and reviews. For information address Balcony Press,
512 E. Wilson Suite 306, Glendale, California 91206.

Caltech's Architectural Heritage: From Spanish Tile to Modern Stone
© 2000 Romy Wyllie

Library of Congress Catalog Card Number: 99-073707
ISBN 1-890449-05-9

CONTENTS

Part One

THE EARLY YEARS

1   Small Beginnings   17
2   New Directions   21

Part Two

BERTRAM GOODHUE

3   Goodhue's Master Plan   31
4   Chemistry and Physics   39
5   Culbertson Hall   53
6   An Untimely Death   61

Part Three

GOODHUE ASSOCIATES

7   A New Relationship   67
8   Chemistry Additions   71
9   Aeronautics   79
10   Humanities   83
11   Astrophysics   93
12   Biology and Geology   107

Part Four

GORDON KAUFMANN

13   The Athenaeum   127
14   Undergraduate Dormitories   143
15   Landscaping the Early Campus   157

Part Five

THE MODERN CAMPUS

16	Changing of the Guard	171
17	Plain and Decorated Boxes	177
18	An Auditorium	185
19	A Central Library	193
20	The Alexander Plan	201
21	The Goldberger Era	209

Part Six

A NEW MASTER PLAN

22	The 1989 Master Plan	217
23	The North Campus	223
24	The South Campus	235
25	Infills and Renovations	241
26	Open Spaces	249
27	The Future	261

	Building Chronology	269
	Acknowledgments	273
	Bibliography	275
	Illustration Credits	276
	Notes	278
	Index	283

FOREWORD

The California Institute of Technology is a small institution with a giant reputation. This is due to many factors, including a belief that superbly talented individuals, given the right resources, excellent colleagues, and a supporting environment, will excel in their pursuit of knowledge. The men who changed Caltech's direction early in this century, Drs. Millikan, Hale, and Noyes, aided by a supportive Board of Trustees, also planned for an institution of architectural distinction. Their successors have tried to add to the campus in ways that would preserve this heritage.

In recent years, a dedicated group of women have contributed their time and talent leading groups of visitors through the campus, explaining Caltech's distinctive architecture. Many alumni who were too busy as students to appreciate the architecture have seen the campus with "new eyes." Prospective students and their parents, faculty and staff, as well as many friends of the Institute have learned a great deal from these volunteers, who comprise the Caltech Architectural Tour Service, affectionately abbreviated to the acronym CATS. To explain the campus architecture in a manner worthy of the Institute, members of CATS have done considerable research on their subject.

It seems very fitting that this research that has been undertaken and shared orally with so many campus visitors in recent years should finally be made available to a larger audience. Romy Wyllie, Missy Jennings and Paula Samazan organized the CATS group in 1985. Romy, who has become an expert on the architectural history of Caltech, graciously agreed to expand the oral tradition to the written word, suitably illustrated to convey the flavor of Caltech's architectural heritage. She has also included some of the landscaping that has improved the environment outside of the buildings. Improved landscaping was suggested, and then supported, by Stephen Bechtel, Jr., one of Caltech's trustees, who believes that people achieve more in a pleasant environment than they would otherwise. Certainly this thought, and this support, have made the campus a very pleasant place to study, to learn, to work, and to do research. Many of our neighbors have also found it a delightful place to walk and to contemplate.

I personally would like to thank Romy for introducing me to some of the rich architectural history of Caltech and for accepting the challenge of writing and assembling the photos for this book. *Caltech's Architectural Heritage* opens a new dimension of appreciation for those who have gone before and will enhance the campus experience for occasional visitors as well as those who spend most days of their life here. Those who read this book will view the campus with new eyes; we all may look forward expectantly to the continuation of the Caltech architectural story, as the Institute enters the next century.

Thomas E. Everhart
President Emeritus

Today Caltech is at an architectural crossroads. We have hired one of the world's great architectural firms, Pei Cobb Fried and Partners, to design a new building which will act as a cornerstone of the North Campus. James Freed is proposing ideas that could take the campus look in subtly new directions. His work should symbolize the optimism the campus feels about the future opportunities opening to Caltech in science, engineering and other aspects of intellectual and artistic life. This is a wonderful time to look back and see where our roots lie.

Romy Wyllie has done Caltech a great service by bringing together a visual history of the campus. Our campus represents the finest of a regional style of American architecture that fuses traditions from other warm, sunny societies — the Spanish, the Italians, the Moors. Walking the campus it feels in places like a monastery, in places like a great European fountained garden — but the whole is subservient to the larger goals of the institution, deep scholarship and wresting truth from behind the veil of nature. Romy has traced for us the origins of this unique and effective environment. Her book is at once a record of remarkable achievement and a challenge to be certain that we honor that achievement as we move forward.

David Baltimore
President

CHAPTER ONE

Small Beginnings

"It is a great undertaking for me at my age but I desired to see it started in my lifetime, and...I wished to use those short days, years,...in putting in operation an institution of public utility... My means are, of course, very limited to found a university but if started right and in a way to meet a public necessity and public favor, it will be maintained...as other institutions have been supported."

— Amos Throop to cousin Cordelia in Iowa, 1892

The roots of the world-renowned California Institute of Technology lie in a small, nascent university created by Amos Gager Throop in 1891.

Amos Throop, the third of seven children, was born in 1811 in New York state. Lacking the opportunity of formal schooling because his parents were poor, Throop learned the meaning of hard work while still a youngster.

Just before his 21st birthday Throop left New York to travel west. He quickly developed a sense of entrepeneurship by saving money from jobs and investing in a variety of projects. After returning to New York to marry, he and his wife Eliza moved to Michigan before settling in Chicago where Throop became a successful businessman and politician. In 1880 the Throops traveled to Los Angeles, invested in a farm, and seven years later bought a home in Pasadena. Then 76 years old, Throop became involved in the affairs of this 5,000 inhabitant community and was elected Mayor.

As a young man Throop had joined the Universalist movement, and later helped establish a church in Chicago before becoming the major benefactor and founder of the first Universalist Church in Pasadena, subsequently renamed Throop Memorial Universalist Church.

In spite of his own lack of education Amos Throop's greatest contribution was to education. Pasadena, which began as a scattering of farms and orchards, had been accessible by rail since 1873 and now had a small business district, a public library and several public and private schools, but no college.

In 1891, Amos Throop established Throop University with an enrollment of 35 students. The purpose of the school is described in its first bulletin, "To furnish students of both sexes and all religious opinions a liberal and practical education, which, while thoroughly Christian, is to be absolutely non-sectarian in its character."

Throop rented space in a large building owned by P. G. Wooster on the corner of

Amos Gager Throop, Caltech's founder. He was known as "Father Throop" because of the valuable contributions he made to Pasadena. He founded the Universalist Church and Throop University, and he was Mayor of the city.

Fair Oaks Avenue and Kansas Street (later renamed Green Street). The building, known as the Wooster block, survives today connected to what remains of Pasadena's grand old Green Hotel. Its massive masonry exterior, enhanced by Romanesque arches and a corner turret, was typical of late nineteenth century commercial construction. The building housed classrooms and a dormitory until 1893, when East Polytechnic Hall and West Hall were constructed on Chestnut Street between Fair Oaks and Raymond Avenues, and adjacent to the original Universalist church founded by Throop.

Although Throop planned a university with the hope of adding a law school, lack of funds and students brought about a new direction. In 1893 he hired Charles H. Keyes as President and changed the school's name to Throop Polytechnic Institute. Throop, who had learned about life through physical labor, regarded the late nineteenth century educational practices as too dependent on books. His educational philosophy was shared by Charles Keyes and was summed up in the school's motto "Learn by Doing."

Amos Throop died in 1894 at the age of 82, leaving a legacy for others to carry on.

The Wooster Building, Throop University's first home. The building still stands on the corner of Fair Oaks Avenue and Green Street. It is connected to what remains of Pasadena's grand old Green Hotel.

New Directions

"To produce skilled and resourceful engineers who are also broadly cultured in the essential humanities is the chief aim of Throop Institute."

— *James A. B. Scherer "The Throop Idea"*

In the next few years Throop Polytechnic's development became more diverse both in its curriculum offerings and the composition of the student body, with the teaching program divided into six separate schools ranging from elementary to college.

A 1902 article titled, "Hand, Eye and Brain," published in *Land of Sunshine*, described a student's first year. "He spends the major part of his time in study of Mathematics, English, the Modern Languages, Latin, Chemistry, Physics, Zoology, Botany, Physiography, Free-hand and Mechanical Drawing. But these branches of learning are applied by daily practice in Carpentry, Wood-turning, Wood-carving, Forging, Pattern-making, Machine Shop Exercises, Cooking, Sewing, and Clay-modelling." In addition chemistry and physics were taught in "expensively equipped laboratories." Tuition for all of the above was listed at $75 a year.

However, the course of Throop Polytechnic's destiny was soon to be altered by a young astronomer named George Ellery Hale. Hale was born in 1868. His father, an elevator manufacturer, taught him to tinker with tools, while his mother encouraged a love of books. He studied physics, chemistry and mathematics at MIT and with his father's help built the Kenwood Observatory in the grounds of his home in Chicago. Before the age of 30 he had invented the spectroheliograph, become director of the Yerkes Observatory in Wisconsin, and founded the *Astrophysical Journal*. In 1902 he was elected to the National Academy of Sciences. Two years later, at the age of 36, Hale succeeded in persuading the Carnegie Institution to fund a solar observatory on Mount Wilson above Pasadena with himself as director.

Hale's youth and energy blended well with the new, fast-growing community of Pasadena. He was instrumental in making a City Beautiful Plan more than a subject for discussion or a drawing on paper. After suggesting an architectural competition, he chaired the jury who selected the architects for the City Hall, Civic Auditorium and Central Library.

Clay Modeling Room and Machine Shop, Throop Polytechnic Institute. Amos Throop felt that traditional education was too dependent on books. In addition to a program of academic studies, students had practical classes which included woodworking, cooking and sewing.

In 1907, three years after establishing the Mount Wilson astronomical observatory, Hale joined Throop Polytechnic's Board of Trustees and quickly persuaded his fellow members to alter the school's multi-faceted program and "concentrate their entire attention on mechanical and electrical engineering" with "adequate instruction in the humanities."

The Institute was as diverse in its curriculum as it was in its roster of Presidents. One of Hale's first jobs as a board member was to find a new leader. Unable to persuade a scientist to accept the challenge, Hale selected James A. B. Scherer, head of Newberry, a small sectarian college in South Carolina. Scherer, who became President in 1909, made up for his lack of scientific training by energetic planning, an ability to raise money, and becoming a voice for the school in articles and speeches. For the *Arroyo Craftsman* he wrote an essay, "The Throop Idea: Character, culture, and good craftsmanship might well spell our creed."

Supervising the divestment of Throop Polytechnic was one of Scherer's early challenges. Shedding all its schools except the college, he reduced the student body by one third, and established it as an all male institution of higher learning. The elementary school moved to the southeast corner of Catalina Avenue and California Boulevard and became the Polytechnic School, now a private co-educational school for ages 6 to 18.

In 1910, as Throop Polytechnic changed its makeup, it left its home in the increasingly crowded area of downtown Pasadena and moved to a 22-acre campus bordered by California Boulevard on the south and San Pasqual Street on the north; Wilson Avenue on the west and Holliston Avenue on the east. The land, planted with orange trees, was a gift from Arthur Fleming, a Canadian of Scottish descent. He had become a citizen of the United States and an attorney in Detroit before moving to California in 1896 where he established one of the largest lumber operations in the old west. As owner of several other companies and a director of the Southern California Edison Company, Fleming amassed a sizeable fortune. He became a Trustee of Throop Polytechnic in 1904. As well as donating the land, he helped to raise money from the citizens of Pasadena for the first building on the new campus. In 1921 he endowed Caltech with his personal fortune retaining only a small annuity for himself.

At the same time that Scherer was establishing Throop Polytechnic in its new home, the state government was considering opening a technical university in southern California to be called the California Institute of Technology. Not wanting a rival college nearby, Scherer, backed by the college trustees, proposed a bill handing over Throop Polytechnic to the state. The bill failed because the state universities in the north did not want to share funding with an upstart in the south and distrusted a college with an independent Board of Trustees. Throop Polytechnic, however, benefited from the publicity and enrollment increased. At this time, Hale offered to work with Scherer to make Throop into "a high-grade institute of technology."

In 1908, the Los Angeles architectural firm of Hunt and Grey was hired to develop a master plan. Myron Hunt had received his architectural education at MIT but Elmer Grey, who was a talented designer and excellent draftsman, had no formal training. Both men had traveled in Europe.

Their brief partnership was formed in 1903 after Hunt had moved to California from Chicago in search of a cure for his wife's tuberculosis.

George Ellery Hale, a brilliant astronomer, administrator and visionary. He came to Pasadena to head the Mount Wilson Observatory. After joining Throop Polytechnic's Board of Trustees in 1907, he persuaded them to change their manual arts training school into a first rate college of engineering. Charcoal sketch by S. Seymour Thomas.

Architects Myron Hunt and Elmer Grey designed Throop Hall and drew up an initial Master Plan for the campus.

Architectural historian Robert Winter, in his monograph *Myron Hunt at Occidental College*, describes Hunt as a good, but not great architect. He was "a business man's architect" who pleased his clients by keeping meticulous records of materials and costs.

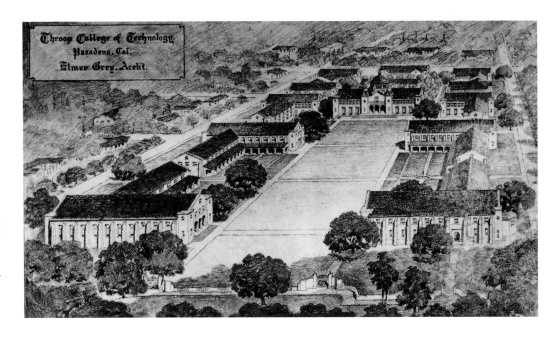

Hunt and Grey's architectural plan. Fourteen buildings flanked a rectangular courtyard. They created a Mission-style campus with Mediterranean overtones: stucco walls, red-tiled roofs, cloisters, and patios. All the buildings would be two stories high except for the central building which, situated on the highest point of the site, would have three stories in the rear.

Throop Hall (originally Pasadena Hall). Hunt wanted an impressive building without a dome but Grey sketched in a dome regardless of the space below. According to one critic, "a dome was necessary to lift this central coronet above its surrounding setting of plain mission structures."

His designs were historical in concept but avoided historical details. Grey added color and creativity to Hunt's solid and functional buildings. But Grey's frills became Hunt's frustration. In describing his partner's design for Throop Hall he wrote, "Mr. Grey took up his pen and drew something in the picture without stopping to consider what the plan beneath might be."

After a tour of college campuses in the eastern United States, Myron Hunt decided to use Thomas Jefferson's design for the University of Virginia as his model for

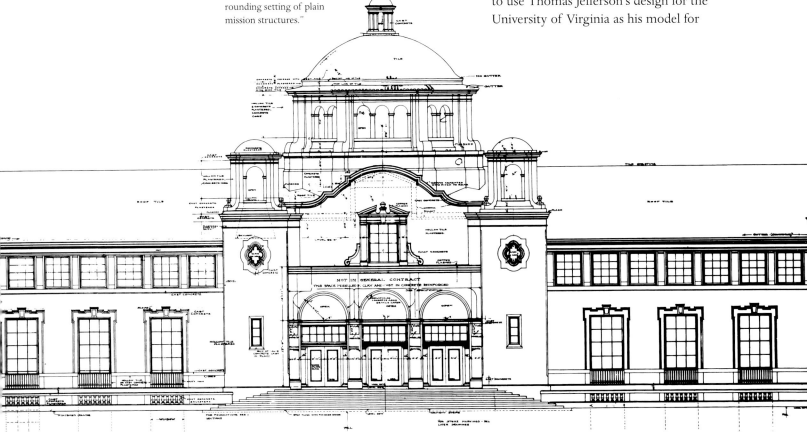

Throop Polytechnic. The Trustees had stated that there were to be fourteen buildings at a cost between two and three million dollars. A plan was to be developed but only one building actually built, not to exceed $26,000. The architects set their fee at five percent of the total cost.

Although Hunt and Grey's plan went through several revisions the theme remained the same. Fourteen buildings flanked a rectangular courtyard. The focus would be on the central building for administrative offices and library which would be perpendicular to the long axis of the court. The architectural style would be Mission with Mediterranean overtones.

On August 10, 1908, at a grand dinner in the Green Hotel, Hale made an eloquent announcement about Throop Polytechnic's first building on its new campus. The design was explained by Hunt and Grey, with the aid of a stereopticon show and sketches displayed on the walls of the dining room. The citizens of Pasadena, inspired by the presentation and urged on by Fleming, raised $160,000 for the building's construction. In their honor it was named Pasadena Hall. In 1920 when the school became the California Institute of Technology, Pasadena Hall was renamed Throop Hall to retain the name of the school's founder.

Initially the facade of the main building was to be like the Ducal palace in Venice with a large shaded arcade below and a skylit library on the top floor. With only administrative offices and a library stipulated the architects were at a loss to know how to plan the rest of the structure. On August 10, 1908, Hunt expressed his frustrations in a letter to Scherer, who was still at Newberry, "We are mentally so constituted as to find ourselves at sea when we do not know the uses to which windows back of a dream are to be put." As soon as he took office Scherer became deeply involved in the plans, making many changes both in the requirements and the design.

Hunt wanted to create an impressive building without using a dome which he felt was "an expensive luxury...and incidentally I do not believe it makes the ideal Library." But Grey sketched in a dome ignoring the space below. Although the concept pleased the Trustees, Hunt was upset because the dome was not a true dome. Later the domed tower room was referred to as "Hunt's Heartache."

In order to make the entrance to the building more imposing Hunt and Grey had recommended that sculptor Alexander Stirling Calder, at that time a Pasadena resident, be asked to design an archway. Calder, the son of a sculptor and father of the inventor of the mobile, had attended the Pennsylvania Academy of Fine Arts and studied at the École des Beaux Arts in Paris. Dr. Norman Bridge, president of the Board of Trustees, dispelled his colleagues' concern that sculptured arches would be too elaborate by offering to pay Calder's commission of $5,000.

Finding the inspiration for his designs in President Scherer's inaugural address, Calder used figures and symbols from mythology to represent the aims and scope of the Institute. In keeping with the Spanish theme of the building the sculptures were confined to an area above the entrance arches, but their style was simplified Beaux Arts rather than Spanish. At the time of their unveiling on February 10, 1910, they were considered one of the most important sculptural projects in Los Angeles.

On June 8 of the same year, the building was officially dedicated. In spite of being disappointed in many aspects of its design (several years later Grey maintained that he was responsible for the exterior design and Hunt for the plan and construction), Hunt was proud of his role. The building was designed to permit re-arrangements of the hollow terra-cotta block partitions. Service pipes and wires fed into the building from an underground conduit which eventually grew into the steam tunnel complex encircling the entire campus.

Entrance to Throop Hall with 1929 freshman class. The archway was designed by sculptor Alexander Stirling Calder. The sculptures are best described in his own words, "Beginning with the spandrel on the left is Nature, in the guise of Pan, piping his gentle joy of life. Flanking this is Art — the poet inscribing his solution of the riddle of life. The left spandrel of the central group represents Energy, bearing the dead away from birds of prey. Then Science, gazing, and lighting his torch at the sun, which forms the central cartouche over the archway. The spandrels over the right archway are winged Imagination, exulting in yet unexplored possibilities; and Law, with watchful preparedness guarding the ancient tablet of the Law, back of which clings gentle Mercy.

"The pilaster decorations between the arches have as motives the sunflower (relating to nature); a terminal bust of Minerva, protectress of the Arts; a terminal bust of Mercury presiding over Science; and on the right the emblem of the Law.

Below the pilasters — a composition representing Life, Death, Eternity, under the sunflower pilaster; Hammer and Anvil below the Science pilaster; a mask below that of Art; while below the Law pilaster is an open book grasped in a hand. The cartouche on the left has been made in the form of a lyre; that in the center, of the life-giving sun, with a border of the signs of the zodiac; and on the right, a great diamond in a setting of lilies and pearls (the rare and precious things of life)."

Throop Hall entry with Apollo statue donated by Louis Bradbury. It is a replica of one in the Vatican Museum made for Bradbury's father. Failing to find a suitable location the elder Bradbury stored the sculpture in an old house used as offices by a Moving Picture company. Poor Apollo was covered in bed sheets because the office girls found the statue offensive.

Throop Hall was officially dedicated on June 8, 1910. At the ceremony, Hunt declared, "..the building which you are dedicating is built for the centuries to come. It has been built proof against fire. There is no wood in its composition save for its doors. Beneath that red tile roof is a concrete roof. The dome is of concrete. The floors, the staircases, are of concrete. The walls are of concrete and unburnable tile. It is fireproof and it is earthquake proof. It is a flexible building. It is an enduring building."

Overlooking the entrance hall of Throop's new building stood a seven-and-a-half foot statue of Apollo loaned to the college by Louis Bradbury, one of Elmer Grey's clients. Bradbury's father had ordered an exact copy made of the Apollo Belvedere after seeing the original in the Vatican Museum. Beloved by generations of students and adorned from time to time in a variety of garments, Apollo spent 30 years in Throop Hall until a remodel of the staircase forced his removal to a balcony between Throop and Kellogg.

Only 31 students and 12 faculty occupied Pasadena Hall at the beginning of its first academic year in 1910. As enrollment increased, civil, mechanical and electrical engineering, physics, humanities, administrative offices, library, bookstore and community cultural center filled the interior space from basement to cupola. On the exterior, Calder's arches became a backdrop and the steps a platform for graduation ceremonies, performances, rallies, and speeches by visiting dignitaries. Throop's new central building remained the nucleus of the campus until its demise in the early 1970s.

Chemistry lab in Throop Hall. Until other buildings were constructed, the hall served the needs of the entire school.

CHAPTER THREE

Goodhue's Master Plan

"THE POSSIBILITY OF UTILIZING ATTRACTIVE ARCHITECTURE TO AROUSE DORMANT PERCEPTIONS WAS NOT OVERLOOKED, AND THE BEST OF ARCHITECTS WAS REQUIRED FOR THE TASK."

— *George Ellery Hale*

Amos Throop had the foresight to establish a place of higher education in Pasadena, but it was George Ellery Hale who took Throop's simple concept and developed it into a broader vision. In addition to proposing the idea of a college dedicated to science and technology, Hale devoted a great deal of his time to raising the necessary funds, hiring the right faculty and finding the best architect. He envisioned a campus planned as an integrated unit with a style of architecture that would blend with the California landscape.

In his essay, "Caltech and Southern California Architecture" Alson Clark states that Hale was disappointed at the "aesthetic failure of Throop Hall." Following completion of this building the partnership of Hunt and Grey collapsed, each architect stating that he would apply separately for projects at Throop Polytechnic. Although Grey was hired to design a chemistry laboratory, Hale was still searching for a master architect with stronger credentials and a bolder vision. He believed that the campus architecture should be an important part of a student's education.

Bertram Grosvenor Goodhue. Hale chose this nationally renowned architect to develop his ideal campus. According to biographer Richard Oliver, this photograph was one of Goodhue's favorites. Denied the opportunity of a university education, he was especially pleased when he was awarded an honorary Doctor of Science by Trinity College in Hartford in 1911.

After viewing the work of Bertram Goodhue at the 1915 Panama-California Exposition in Balboa Park, San Diego, Hale decided he had found his man. He was particularly impressed with the true Spanish spirit and exoticism expressed in Goodhue's Exposition buildings, "Seeing this, and realizing at once that its creator was a pure

genius, I urged the trustees ...to profit by
their opportunity."

Bertram Grosvenor Goodhue was born
on April 28, 1869 in Pomfret, Connecticut of
Anglo-American heritage. Although
Goodhue's parents were educated and gen-
teel, they lacked the necessary funds to send
their son to a university. Goodhue made up
for the lack of a formal education by reading
and sketching prodigiously, having inherited
a natural artistic ability from his mother. He
is described as, "slight, blond, blue-eyed, red-
cheeked and debonair." At the age of 15 he
apprenticed in an architect's office in New
York City where he became an excellent
draftsman. At the same time he indulged an
inclination to create fanciful drawings of
imaginary cities with romantic names.
Influenced by the works of William Morris,

Goodhue also designed book covers, book-
plates and fonts. Like other architects of the
period he found inspirations for his work
from visits to countries such as Canada,
Mexico, Germany, Persia, India and China.

Work at a Boston architectural firm led to
the partnership of Cram, Goodhue and
Ferguson and a leading role in ecclesiastical
design. After Goodhue opened his own office
in New York City he designed churches,
cathedrals, libraries, university campuses, military bases, town plans, commercial buildings, and residences. Although considered a
revivalist, Goodhue took the best of traditional forms, simplifying and reworking them
with uninhibited freedom. In his later work
he strove to break away from historicism in
an effort to develop a more innovative and
individual style. At the beginning of the

A bird's eye view of Goodhue's Master Plan. Flanking a grand entrance on Wilson Avenue would be an Auditorium and Art Museum on the south and a Science Museum on the north. Administrative offices would remain in Pasadena Hall (later renamed Throop Hall), with two buildings on either side devoted to lectures. Across the central plaza from Pasadena Hall would be a Memorial building to serve as the dominant element of the entire campus. On the north side of the central plaza would be the Chemistry and Physics group with unassigned buildings adjoining the Physics group to the Science Museum. On the south side Goodhue located Electrical and Civil Engineering. Behind Pasadena Hall would be a Gymnasium facing a long secondary court flanked by Engineering buildings on either side. At the eastern end of the plot would be three dormitory buildings.

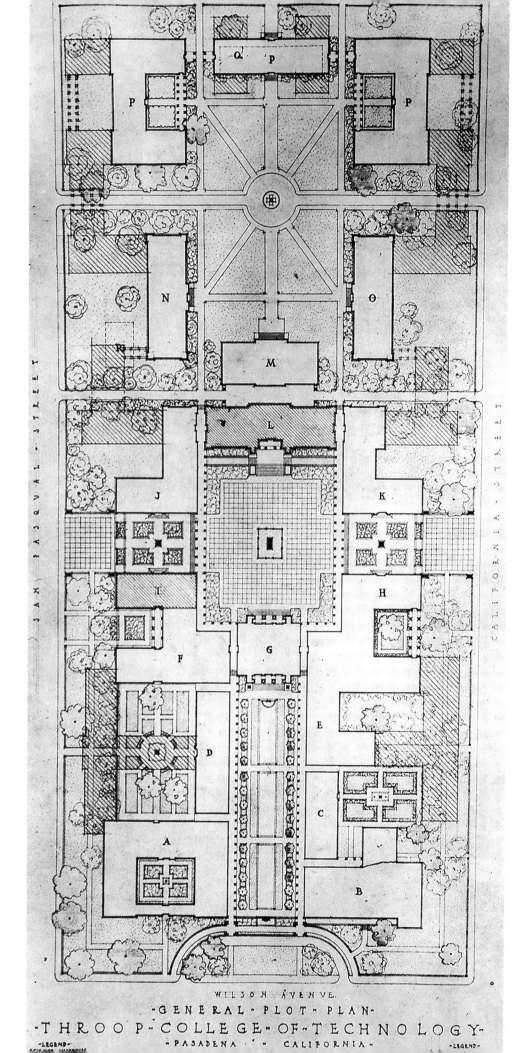

WILSON AVENUE.

-GENERAL·PLOT·PLAN-

-THROOP·COLLEGE·OF·TECHNOLOGY-

-PASADENA·-·CALIFORNIA-

·MEMORIAL BVILDING FROM S.E. CORNER OF PLAZA·

A sketch of the Memorial Building from the southeast corner of the main Plaza. Using an urban setting as his model, Goodhue strengthened Hunt and Grey's axial arrangement by aligning his buildings on either side of the east-west pathway. The rigidity of the axes would be broken by occasional courtyards with a central paved area, 180 feet square, at the intersection of the two main axes. Like plazas in Spanish cities or the central quadrangle of a Spanish university, this square could be used for gatherings or, with seating set up for 6500, for graduations.

twentieth century he was considered a great architect but appreciation for his work has diminished over time.

In 1913 Throop Polytechnic Institute became Throop College of Technology with a 22-acre campus, a temporary wooden dormitory, and an academic building that stood alone on a dry, scrubby slope against a backdrop of decrepit orange trees which gave off intoxicating perfumes. During World War I trenches, which were used for military instruction and exercises, were scattered around the grounds. When Goodhue first visited the campus in 1916 the setting was a far cry from the ivy-covered walls and tree-filled quadrangles of the eastern college which had inspired Myron Hunt. After some concern about having two independent architects working on the campus at the same time, the Trustees hired Goodhue to develop a master plan and serve as consultant for the design of the Chemistry building.

During his long train journeys across the country Goodhue wrote detailed letters to Hale, Scherer and Fleming expressing his ideas and plans for the California campus. With Scherer he discussed the fundamentals of the Block Plan: the placement and heights of buildings, ground levels, landscaping and driveways. Scherer explained that the academic buildings must be "elastic" to meet unknown and changing functions and that the existing oak trees should "virtually govern the layout of the buildings." With Hale Goodhue had lengthy discussions on the aesthetics of the scheme, in particular whether the ornamentation should follow the "Plateresque" or "Churrigueresque" style. Plateresque, from the Spanish word for silver, refers to detailed carvings with low relief similar to metalsmiths' intricate designs found on buildings of the early Renaissance period. Churrigueresque, named after a family of architects called Churriguera, has bolder carvings with deeper relief and is more typical of the later Renaissance years. On March 2, 1916, Hale wrote to Goodhue, "What I mean is a true fusion of Gothic and Spanish, leaving out the more lace-like elements of the Plateresque." In general Goodhue adhered to Hale's suggestions although many of his buildings have columns and windows decorated with lambrequins, an overlapping scalloped shape which is associated with the Plateresque.

A 14-page report (undated but probably written in 1917) accompanied Goodhue's general Block Plan, a bird's eye view of the proposed campus and several sketches of buildings and courtyards. In the same spirit of Hunt and Grey's master plan, Goodhue wanted to establish form and structure for the campus. The site was to be divided into six areas: Artistic, Scientific, Administrative, Engineering, Athletic and Residential.

In order to unify the campus, provide an outward appearance of similarity, and give shelter and shade Goodhue would link his academic buildings with arcades "or, as the Spanish call them, portales." He stated that the flat roofs of the arcades would serve as fire escapes or galleries for viewing academic processions. Walls, arbors and landscaped spaces would separate town and gown and discourage the public from wandering onto the campus grounds.

In order to establish the Spanish character of the buildings, Goodhue proposed following a principle of Moorish architecture in which long expanses of plain wall were contrasted with the massing of ornament around important doorways and windows. In the same Moorish context Goodhue suggested that cast stone wall carvings would contrast with brightly colored glazed tiles around fountains and on domes. However, Goodhue felt free to play with different historical styles intermingling Romanesque and Byzantine with Gothic or Spanish. He says, "We have not hesitated to employ features from other styles and other lands when such seemed desirable and harmonious."

Pasadena Hall posed a serious problem for Goodhue because the design did not conform to his interpretation of Spanish architecture. Like Hunt, Goodhue was bothered by the fact that the dome was "false, in that it does not follow down through the building." In fact Hunt's heartache became Goodhue's headache. In letters to Scherer he proposed enlarging the dome, covering it with tile and removing the rooms below so that the dome would be visible from a rotunda on the first floor. To make up for the lost floor space he suggested adding a story by raising the roof on the north and south ends. But Scherer had no sympathy with Goodhue's desire to tamper with Pasadena Hall. He urged Goodhue to do the best he could with "this fixed condition," and on December 10, 1915 he wrote, "We might end up exchanging a beautiful building for a monstrosity."

In spite of this reaction Goodhue repeated his suggestions to change Pasadena Hall in his Block Plan Report explaining that the building lacked height and presence and would be out of balance across from his proposed, and much grander Memorial Building. This central building served two purposes: its location closed off the western edge of the central square, and it provided Goodhue with an architectural focal point. The building, its use as yet undetermined, would be topped by a resplendent blue-tiled dome visible from every corner of the campus.

Between the Memorial Building and Wilson Avenue, Goodhue designed a long courtyard with a reflecting pool down its central axis and cypress trees flanking the arcades on either side. Crossing the pool would be two "bunds," an Indian term meaning part-bridge part-dam which would allow the water to be at different levels according to the grading of the land. Goodhue, ever the romantic, visualized a ceremonial march of faculty in academic regalia with spectators watching from the shaded arcades. Entering from Wilson Avenue the procession would pass alongside the pool, "through the great central archway of the Memorial Building to the Plaza and its tribune" beyond.

Detail of the Memorial Building. In a letter to President Scherer, dated December 9, 1916, Goodhue described the courtyard which would form the approach from Wilson Avenue to the domed building, "The central long court leading up to the Memorial Building ..will give..one of the most effective things of the kind I know and with its portales, rows of cypresses, garden and central pool of water, something, though on a smaller scale, of the effect of the one leading to the Taj Mahal at Agra."

Chemistry and Physics

While President Scherer focused on the management of the school and raising funds, Hale worked at building up its faculty. It took many meetings, a two-year part-time teaching appointment and the promise of a new building for Hale to persuade Arthur Amos Noyes to break a long and strong bond with MIT and become head of the Division of Chemistry at Throop College of Technology. Like Hale, Noyes believed in the importance of research in pure science, and that to be thoroughly educated scientists should study the humanities.

On March 10, 1916, ground was finally broken for Noyes' promised chemistry laboratory. The building was named for the principal contributors, Charles and Peter Gates, Pasadena businessmen, who had made their money in lumber. Arthur Fleming paid for equipment and an annual maintenance income.

The 18,000 square foot building would contain offices, a lecture room, large and small laboratories, chemical stock rooms and a library with Professor Noyes' office in the southwest corner of the first floor.

Goodhue suggested locating the new structure, now called the Gates Chemistry Laboratory, to the north-west of Throop Hall, near San Pasqual where it would help to form the layout of his central square. He agreed with Scherer's suggestion to move it 12 feet closer to Throop Hall so that its long axis would be centered on Michigan Avenue, a north-south street intersecting San Pasqual Street.

Elmer Grey was the principal architect of the laboratory but Hale asked Bertram Goodhue to design the exterior. Fortunately Grey and Goodhue, who already knew each other and were good friends, cooperated amicably. Hunt and Grey's master plan had made Throop Hall, sitting on an elevated site, the highest building on the campus with a two-story, chemistry laboratory at a lower level. But Goodhue tried to persuade Grey to raise the height of Chemistry because he wanted the buildings flanking his central courtyard or "Court of Honour" to have more presence. Scherer ended the discussion by prohibiting any competition with Throop Hall.

Arthur Amos Noyes. In 1919 he left MIT to head the newly formed chemistry division at Throop College.

Goodhue's rendering of Gates Laboratory of Chemistry with the Memorial Building dome in the background. To strengthen his Spanish Renaissance theme, Goodhue used baroque ornamentation called Churrigueresque. The style is named for the Churrigueras, a family of Spanish architects.

The triumvirate, George Ellery Hale, Arthur Amos Noyes, and Robert Andrews Millikan, in front of Gates Laboratory of Chemistry. Underneath the double stairway is one of Goodhue's many charming fountains with a head and shell design above the basin.

Although Goodhue was not responsible for the Gates chemistry laboratory plan and interior, his revision of Grey's "frontispiece, fenestration and cornice" established the Spanish Renaissance decoration which Hale had designated as the overall theme for the campus. He retained Grey's arrangement of doors and windows but made his ornamental balconies functional. Goodhue also added his own embellishments consisting of interpenetrating lambrequin shapes under the windows, a rope design framing the cornice and an elaborate Churrigueresque style carving of shells, spirals, and leaf-entwined columns framing a grand entry door made of ornamental iron work.

All of Goodhue's ornamental stone work was made from "cast stone," an artificial sandstone-like material formed by cement-casting sand in molds. The decorations for the Gates Laboratory were prepared from models made by a Mr. Piccirilli who

Goodhue refers to as "his pet modeller here in New York." The Piccirilli family were in fact well known sculptors and stone cutters and responsible for several of New York's civic monuments.

To the south of the building Goodhue and Grey cooperated in the design of an arcade using a style of column found at Mission San Juan Capistrano. Goodhue changed Grey's three arches to five and replaced Grey's plaster ceiling with wood beams. These Spanish portales would be extended as other buildings were constructed.

Noyes' new laboratory was completed in 1917, but it was not until 1919 that he broke his ties with MIT and took a full-time position at Throop College.

Physics

"The architectural beauty of the building does contribute in a large way to the 'mental health, power, and pleasure' of those working in it, and should be a large factor in creating the proper atmosphere for real creative work such as it is hoped the laboratory will foster."

— *Earnest C. Watson. October, 1925*

Robert Andrews Millikan. He was responsible for creating one of the best known physics departments in the country, and was chairman of the Executive Council from 1920 to 1946.

As early as 1912 Hale had hoped that the Carnegie Foundation would add to the Mount Wilson Observatory project by funding physical chemistry and physics laboratories in Pasadena. But his hopes were dashed when the Carnegie Foundation experienced financial problems. By 1917, with a chemistry laboratory completed and a director designated, Hale (urged on by Noyes) renewed his efforts to find the funding for a physics division. Both men agreed that Robert Millikan was the obvious choice, but an inducement in the form of a laboratory with assurance of money for research would be needed.

Robert Andrews Millikan was born in 1868 in Illinois where his father was a Congregational Minister. After obtaining his doctorate in physics from Columbia, he studied at the Universities of Berlin and Göttingen before joining the faculty at the University of Chicago. In 1917, just before America entered World War I, Millikan agreed to spend three months a year at Throop College. He was appointed director of physical research and began a series of public lectures.

In 1920, with the war over and the school's educational program now encompassing chemistry and physics in addition to engineering, the leaders decided that the California Institute of Technology was a more appropriate name than Throop College of Technology.

To help make the expansion into physics a reality, Trustee Dr. Norman Bridge had agreed to provide the funds for a complex of three buildings. Dr. Bridge had practiced and taught medicine in Chicago before moving to Southern California where he turned his assets into a fortune by investing in oil exploration. In Pasadena he promoted music, art and education, and helped establish La Viña Sanatorium. He was President of Throop's Board of Trustees for many years.

Goodhue's early plans located a physics building on the north side of the campus to prevent the vibration of trolley cars on California Boulevard from interfering with delicate machinery. Located next to the Gates Chemistry Laboratory, it would have butted up to the Science Museum on the west and the Memorial Building on the

Bridge Laboratory of Physics 1922-1924. The first unit, East Bridge is a fine example of Goodhue's sense of balance and proportion. Between the rectangular upper windows he placed medallions representing Fire, Water, Earth and Air, the four essential components of all matter according to the ancient Greek philosophers Heracleitus and Empedocles. Similar panels of double medallions on West Bridge symbolize modern science: one medallion represents the Compton effect (the scattering effect of electrons), the other the structure of the carbon atom.

Tower of East Bridge. On one side of the tower a plain wall is enlivened with 18 elongated quatrefoil-shaped windows set like jewels into an overall repetitive motif called a diaper design. The same Moorish-inspired pattern is repeated on the north and west facades so that the building would relate to the Memorial Building with its tiled dome overlooking the central court.

Bridge Annex with two distillation flasks below an arch. The geometrical stone lattice-work filling the arch is similar to mashrabiyya grilles used in Muslim architecture to provide privacy but allow breezes to cool the interior.

south. But when it became necessary to enlarge the package to attract Millikan, Goodhue suggested that an area south of Throop Hall parallel to California Boulevard would provide ample space for several buildings. The new plan consisted of an open court, which would be flanked by a U-shaped physics complex on the west side and a High Potential Research Laboratory on the east side.

The physics group, built between 1920 and 1924, represents the essence of Goodhue's academic buildings. East Bridge, asymmetrical but perfectly proportioned, has strong horizontal lines interrupted by a vertical entry tower whose upper windows are decorated with Churrigueresque and lambrequin ornamentation. The two buildings flanking the "U" of the physics group are three stories high with two floors below ground, but the joining annex, which runs parallel to the central court, has only one story to permit the dome of the Memorial Building to be viewed from the street.

The construction is reinforced concrete with the columns, outside walls and floor slabs carrying the weight. Interior partitions of hollow tile free of wiring or piping could be removed or additional walls could be added. The main lecture hall seated 260 people and was lit by a skylight with motorized curtains. Earnest C. Watson, who began a public lecture series which continues today, was hired in 1920 to supervise the construction of the buildings. Students in electrical engineering installed the electrical wiring and equipment. For the convenience of scientists who wished to play tennis during the day, two showers and a dressing-room were installed in the sub-basement.

In order to create continuity between the academic buildings Goodhue designed the first floor corridors with similar features and materials: padre tile floors, vaulted ceilings, decorative light fixtures, wrought-iron stair railings and doors opening onto important rooms, and water fountains set in marble basins surrounded with faience tile in a variety of designs and colorful glazes. East Bridge sets the standard for other buildings on campus. Opposite the entrance and double staircase, a wrought-iron door crowned by the newly created initials of the California Institute of Technology opens

Drinking Fountains in East and West Bridge add to the Spanish ambiance of Goodhue's designs. The marble basins are surrounded with faience tile in a variety of designs and colorful glazes.

Detail of lambrequins.
Delicate overlapping
lambrequins flowed down
from the top of piers
breaking up their scale.

onto a reading room with a central light
fixture in the form of a medallion of the
four elements. The central library of the
Institute, moved from under the dome in
Throop Hall, filled the annex between East
and West Bridge. Many years later it was
divided into offices, and its decorative
beamed ceiling destroyed.

In 1921, with the physics laboratories
under construction, research funds found
and equipment promised, Millikan agreed to
move permanently to California.

When Hale realized that a laboratory
dedicated to high voltage research might be
the deciding factor in persuading Millikan to
join the Caltech faculty, he devised "the
Edison scheme." Hale's plan, in which the
Southern California Edison Company would
help to fund a laboratory in return for using
its facilities, was supported by Trustees
Fleming and Robinson, both of whom were
directors of Edison.

Caltech's bulletin of December 1923 stated, "It (High Volts) will be available both for
the pursuit of special scientific problems
connected with the structure of matter and
the nature of radiation, and for the conduct
of the pressing engineering problems having
to do with the improvement in the art of
high tension transmission." Although such a
cooperative effort was unusual the effort
paid off. The February 1949 issue of

High Volts Building from California Avenue. Goodhue covered the exterior walls in a diamond-shaped diaper pattern to detract from the absence of windows. Although Goodhue refers to Moorish architecture as his inspiration, similar patterns are also found on Mayan ruins, in particular those in Uxmal where the walls of several buildings are decorated with repetitive geometric shapes.

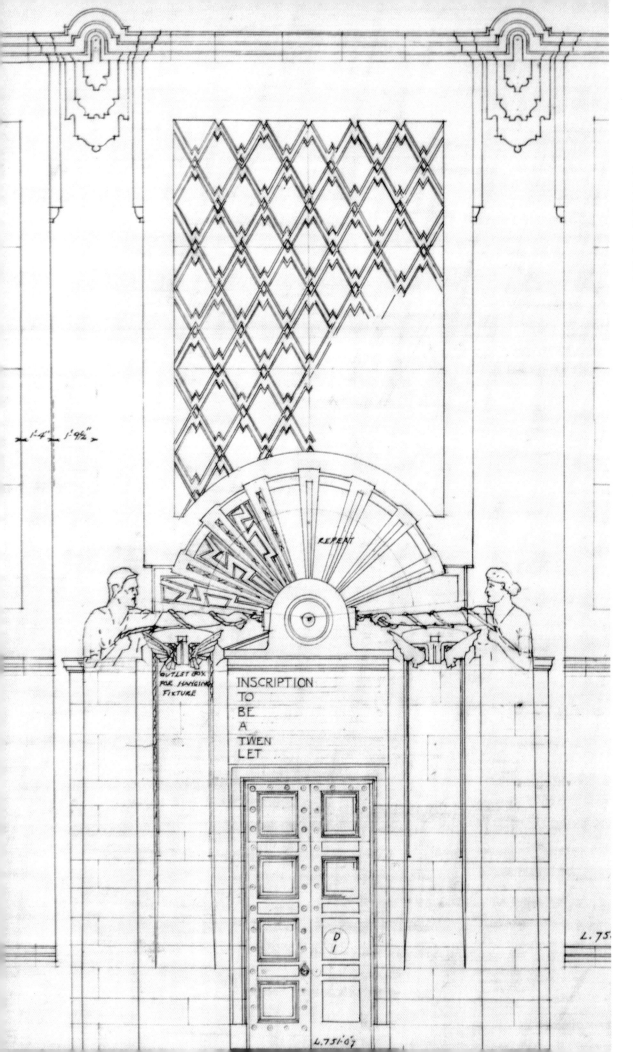

High Volts entrance. Goodhue's sculptor, Lee Lawrie, originally showed a drawing of a man and a woman with extended arms holding a cable and creating a powerful discharge of electricity.

Perhaps because Caltech was an all male institution the sculpture over the door was changed to two men, mirror images of each other.

REPEAT

OUTLET BOX
FOR HANGING
FIXTURE

INSCRIPTION
TO
BE
A
TWEN
LET

1'4"   1'9½"

L. 75

D
I

L.751·07

Engineering and Science described the early work in High Volts, "The first laboratory in the country to have a reliable one million volt power frequency, provided by a chain system of transformers designed by Professor Sorensen (who had been hired in 1909 as the school's first instructor in electrical engineering)...These facilities have been used to aid Southern California Edison in the development of high voltage transmission lines, (enabling them to bring power to Southern California from the Hoover Dam), to furnish lightning protection of oil storage tanks for the oil industry, to test insulators for numerous utility companies."

The final cost of the building was $139,915. Southern California Edison provided $105,000 and the Institute paid the balance. Alternately called the Edison High Tension Laboratory and the High Voltage Research Laboratory, it became known affectionately as "High Volts."

In a letter to Goodhue dated February 10, 1922, Millikan made sure that the interior space would be suitable for the high powered work planned for it. "There must be a minimum clearance of 47 feet between the floor and the roof truss in order that the high potential discharge may not pass to the building; this means about 56 feet from the top of the building to the floor. An inside width of 58 feet will give the required clearance for a million volts." The letter went on to explain the need for ventilation to allow ozone gas to escape but at the same time it must be light-tight. The final size of the building was 50 feet high, 60 feet wide and 100 feet long. The construction consisted of a steel frame set on 9 foot wide footings to offset the absence of floors. The frame, designed by the Edison engineers, was only the second one made of steel to be used in Pasadena.

To offset the plain industrial interior, Goodhue designed a decorative exterior. He covered the walls in a diamond-shaped diaper pattern to detract from the absence of windows, and lightened the visual weight of the piers with overlapping lambrequins. A sculpture over the entry door of two men holding a cable to create an arc of electricity symbolized the purpose of the building.

After the completion of High Volts and Bridge Physics, arcades were built to connect the buidings and form the southern edge of the central courtyard. The arcades terminated in a wall with a tiled fountain outside the Bridge Annex building. At the northern end of the court between High Volts and East Bridge another small fountain with a bronze background was set into the wall below the arcades. Both of these fountains have since been removed.

The spigot of a small fountain which once stood in front of the arcade wall between East Bridge and High Volts.

CHAPTER FIVE

Culbertson Hall

"In 1910 a group of men and women in Pasadena became actively interested in the establishment and maintenance of a hall of music and other arts, beautiful and permanent in character, which should afford a place suitable for the appearance of the greatest musical artists and for the display of the work of the best painters and sculptors."

— *President Scherer. Annual Report 1911–1912*

Between 1920 and 1921, during the construction of East Bridge, a small auditorium was built to serve the needs of the Institute and the city. In his 1911-12 annual report President Scherer had explained the concept of the hall and announced that Throop would offer space on its new campus.

Elmer Grey began work on the design of a Music Auditorium in 1913. The building would face Wilson Avenue with an attached Art Museum wing parallel to California Boulevard. Following the death in 1915 of James A. Culbertson, Vice President of Throop's Board of Trustees, it was decided to name the hall in his honor.

When Goodhue began work on the master plan Hale asked him to take over the auditorium project. Goodhue increased the seating capacity from 1100 to 1400, changed Grey's rectangular Art Museum into a small square reception wing, and estimated the total cost at $200,000. As with other areas of the campus plan, Hale was outspoken in his ideas for its design. He stipulated that the hall be academic in feeling without being too cold or solemn. He encouraged Goodhue to combine Gothic and Spanish influences and to use color or possibly a decorative frieze.

From the inception of the idea that the city and the college would share the space, a building fund had been established. The Pasadena Music and Art Association Ladies, together with influential citizens and social leaders, organized a series of concerts to raise money. Although two anonymous donors, later identified as Miss Kate Fowler (Fleming's sister-in-law) and her niece Marjorie Fleming Lloyd-Smith (Fleming's daughter) promised $25,000 each, insufficient funds were raised to build the entire complex. Nevertheless, by mid-1920 it was decided to proceed with construction of the wing making it into a multi-use hall which would eventually become the reception annex for the larger building on Wilson Avenue.

The small box-like building had plain walls broken on two sides by a group of high windows. A wooden entrance door

Grey's rendering of a
garden and Art Museum
which would have formed
a court behind the pro-
posed Music Auditorium
facing Wilson Avenue.

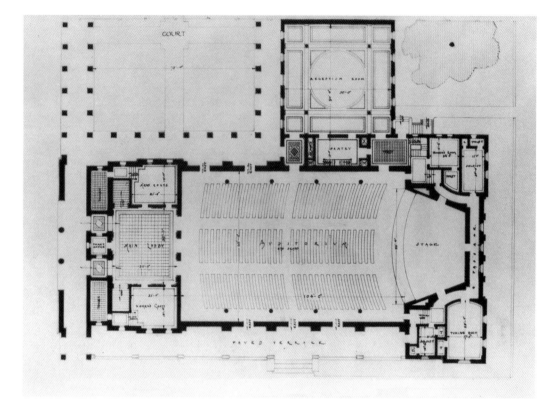

Goodhue's Plan for a Music Auditorium to be named for James Culbertson. Only enough money was raised to build the small reception wing (on the east side, top of plan). This became Culbertson Hall.

Sketch of Goodhue's Music Auditorium. The building stood parallel to Wilson Avenue extending from the West Court to California Boulevard.

1922 Aerial view of the campus with Throop Hall, Gates Laboratory of Chemistry, East Bridge (the first building of the physics complex,) and Culbertson Hall. The playing field and stands, where the Tournament of Roses games were originally played, can be seen on the south side of California Boulevard.

decorated with metal studs was illuminated by a single wrought iron fixture. In contrast the hall's interior exploded with richness and warmth. A trussed ceiling of Oregon pine with a central vault decorated in square and octagonal-shaped carved panels covered the main auditorium space. Following the suggestion of Miss Fowler the 500 seats could be removed and, as Goodhue explained, the four structural columns would not interfere with dancing. However, in 1937 these large square columns were replaced with smaller round ones.

For fifty years Culbertson Hall provided a home for community concerts, academic lectures, and students performances. By 1972 two larger auditoriums had been built on campus and the space where Culbertson stood was needed for a new seismology laboratory.

When the building was demolished only a few of the interior treasures were saved. Unfortunately the Panel of the Nine Muses, which had decorated the top of the proscenium arch, embarked on a fateful journey. President Harold Brown agreed to a five-year loan with a possible extension to the Bohemian Club of San Francisco for display at their Pelican Camp in Monte Rio. Although the delicate plaster of Paris bas-relief had been coated with a protective polymer before leaving Caltech, it suffered a transverse crack in transit. After a sculptor in San Francisco made a new fiberglass cast, the original was destroyed. Currently, efforts are underway to have the recast frieze returned to the campus.

CHAPTER SIX

An Untimely Death

"I LOVED AND ADMIRED HIM AS A GREAT MAN AND SINCERE FRIEND AS WELL AS A GREAT ARCHITECT."

— *George Ellery Hale*

During the period that Goodhue was involved with the campus design for Caltech, his creative genius was much in demand. He maintained a heavy workload at his office in New York City, and he traveled to various destinations to oversee his projects. Goodhue was a tireless and dedicated designer. He never rested or took time off for leisure activities. Even when spending a Sunday with his family at his west coast retreat in Montecito, he always wore a tie and starched collar.

Other projects on the drawing boards in Goodhue's New York office included a central library for Los Angeles, a capitol building for Nebraska (regarded as Goodhue's finest work), and a headquarters building for the National Academy of Sciences in Washington, D.C.. Goodhue had accepted the commission even though it might require him to conform to the Beaux Arts architecture of Washington. In the end he succeeded in designing an elegant marble building whose symmetry and implied pilasters acknowledged the classicism of other buildings nearby without conforming to all their traditional elements.

The dedication of the Academy building was to take place on April 28, 1924, Goodhue's 55th birthday. Five days before the event, Goodhue suffered a heart attack and died.

In commemoration of Goodhue and his contribution to the campus, the Trustees agreed to have a fountain built in the U-shaped courtyard formed by the Bridge buildings. Lee Lawrie, who was commissioned to design the memorial, insisted on donating his services. Unfortunately he was busy with other projects and was unable to complete the design and its model for several years. On December 9, 1931, the Executive Council reviewed the design and expressed their approval but postponed construction because "the financial condition of the Institute is such that it cannot go ahead with the Goodhue fountain." Millikan wrote to Phillips (one of the Goodhue Associates), "Lawrie's sketch is a wonderfully beautiful thing, and it is a crime that it cannot be made a reality now."

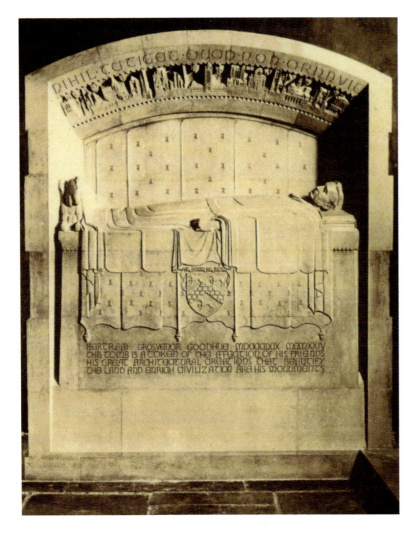

Regrettably, the Memorial fountain never became a reality. However, there is a small memorial on the south face of West Bridge in the form of a medallion containing the Goodhue family coat of arms. Goodhue had used this same shield in the composition of his personal bookplate, and Lee Lawrie incorporated it into the design of Goodhue's tomb in the Chapel of the Intercession, New York City. At the time of Goodhue's death West Bridge was under construction and it is possible that the members of his firm suggested replacing one of the science medallions with a tribute to their master architect.

The eight year period during which Goodhue worked on Caltech's master plan proved to be an important chapter in his career. After his success as a Gothic revivalist followed by projects using themes from Spanish Renaissance and Spanish Colonial, Goodhue began to free himself from the restrictions of historical reference. His architectural language became simpler and his forms bolder. Abstract and geometric motifs foreshadowed the designs of art deco.

The four corner buildings of Caltech's central courtyard represent Goodhue's

View of Goodhue's tomb in the Chapel of the Intercession, New York City. Lee Lawrie, Goodhue's devoted sculptor, donated the model and friends raised funds for its construction. The memorial was unveiled on Palm Sunday, March 24, 1929. Lawrie placed the family coat of arms beneath Goodhue's hand.

Photographs of Lee Lawrie's model of the proposed Goodhue Memorial Fountain. Plans for its installation between East and West Bridge buildings were cancelled because of lack of funds.

architectural progression. The elaborate Churrigueresque decoration of Gates Chemistry is an example of Goodhue's involvement with historicism in the guise of Spanish Renaissance; East Bridge (Physics) shows Goodhue's mastery of proportions and a more restrained use of decoration; the architecture of High Volts focusses on its structural order with delicate ornamentation on the walls and pilasters in contrast to the bold sculptural figures framing the entrance; Dabney Hall of the Humanities, which was completed by Goodhue's firm after his death, embodies Goodhue's last and most mature style using forms found in pueblo architecture with abstract decoration inspired by Mayan designs.

Although the Memorial Building and its reflecting pool were never built, the core of Goodhue's Master Plan had been established before his death. His aim "to provide the atmosphere of scholarly calm and classic shade ever associated with the academic life" was fulfilled by integrating landscape and architecture. The flexibility of the buildings was achieved through a simple and uniform architectural style with loft-like interiors which could be configured in a variety of ways. Adjacent structures had interiors linked by continuous corridors and exteriors by arcades. Although the fronts of the academic buildings created the borders of the axes, their backs looked onto courtyards allowing space for expansion.

Goodhue memorial medallion on the south facade of West Bridge. It also features the Goodhue family coat of arms surrounded by their motto, "Nec Invideo, Nec Despicio (Neither Envy, Nor Despise)." The dates are 1869-1924.

Bertram Grosvenor Goodhue

Goodhue's Spanish Renaissance theme was expressed through skillful use of dissimilar elements: elaborate ornamentation contrasted with plain walls; open plazas with intimate patios; and a magnificent central building with simple academic laboratories.

According to Hale, "Goodhue was generally regarded as the ablest and most original architect in the country at the time of his death." In 1925, the American Institute of Architects awarded Goodhue its Gold Medal posthumously, and published a commemorative book on his work. Hale, who was one of the essayists wrote, "The possibilities of planted patio and shaded portale, of rich decoration concentrated in the Spanish way, of iron grills [sic] and brilliant tiles, of sheltering walls and Persian pools, were not neglected in Goodhue's design for the California Institute...his scheme remains for future guidance, and the trustees of the Institute may be depended upon to carry it step by step to ultimate completion."

CHAPTER SEVEN

A New Relationship

"It is some gratification to feel that with his [Goodhue's] death there does not perish the fresh creation of architectural beauty of a kind that he so long taught."

— *Gano Dunn to Robert Millikan, 1924*

Originally Hale had wanted Throop Polytechnic to be a first rate college of engineering, but as the academic program developed he realized the importance of putting pure science in the forefront. Astronomer Hale, chemist Noyes, and physicist Millikan had become firm friends through their World War I work establishing the National Research Council as an important branch of the National Academy of Sciences. After the war was over this powerful triumvirate put their collaborative efforts into making the newly named California Institute of Technology the best place for scientific research on the west coast.

Noyes had committed himself to a full time position at the Institute in 1919, and Millikan made the move in 1921 agreeing at the same time to be Chairman (he refused to be called President) of the Executive Council. Scherer, worn out by his responsibilities and the struggle to raise funds, had resigned in 1920.

Millikan, a gifted teacher, a brilliant scientist and energetic administrator, was determined to make his new base at Caltech the best known physics department in the country. Money and an ability to discover quality researchers enabled him to achieve his ambition. In her book *Millikan's School*, Caltech archivist Judith Goodstein explained that "Hale and Noyes promised Millikan the lion's share of the school's financial resources." In 1923 Millikan's own research efforts were rewarded with the Nobel Prize in Physics for isolating the electron and measuring its charge.

However, Caltech was committed to more subjects than physics. Noyes wanted to expand chemistry. Two more buildings would give his division the same U-shaped complex on the north side of the central square as physics had on the south side. And in the next few years humanities, aeronautics, astrophysics, biology, and geology would need homes.

Bertram Goodhue's unexpected death left Caltech's leaders feeling uncertain as to how to proceed with the architectural scheme. Gano Dunn, chairman of the

National Academy's building committee, tried to reassure Millikan that Goodhue's associates, Francis L. S. Mayers, Oscar H. Murray and Hardie Phillip, were quite capable of carrying on their master's work. In August of 1924 he wrote to Millikan, "Evidently it is a case where a real genius knew how to surround himself with other men of genius in the artistic sphere and men of level business and executive heads in the practical sphere — an unusual combination."

Over a period of fifteen years the Goodhue Associates, later renamed Mayers, Murray and Phillip, completed eleven more buildings of Bertram Goodhue's original scheme for Caltech. Eager to assuage any concerns on the part of clients, Francis Mayers wrote, "We have got a tradition so great as to make us almost tremble when we think of living up to it; but if our reputation is to be worth anything, it must be on the basis of showing to the world that our master's teachings have not been in vain."

In spite of such good intentions difficulties arose. Hale, who had shared a special relationship with Goodhue, failed to develop the same connection with Hardie Phillip. The bi-coastal distance inhibited communication, and the partners were unable to spend as much time as Goodhue had traveling around the country to meet with individual clients and oversee projects.

Hale wrote to Fleming in October, 1927, "Our distance from New York and consequent inability to hold frequent conferences with our architects are getting us deeper and deeper into difficulty." He became especially frustrated over deviations from the original Spanish character of the master plan, "It should be a perfectly simple matter for the Goodhue Associates to give us the benefit, not of their individual conceptions or of any impressions they may have as to the manner in which Mr. Goodhue might have modified his design, but of his actual design, as approved by him and accepted by us." Hale appreciated that some details might have to be modified because of changing requirements, but he was determined not to lose the spirit of the original Spanish Colonial concept. "I do mean that the style of the domed building, as shown in the perspective, should determine the style of the buildings bordering the pools."

Arthur Amos Noyes,
Robert Andrews Millikan,
George Ellery Hale. This
portrait by Seymour
Thomas hangs in the main
dining room of Caltech's
Athenaeum.

CHAPTER EIGHT

Chemistry Additions

"DR. HALE SAYS — GET SOME CHARM INTO IT, SOME OF THE SPANISH FEATURES THAT MAKE THAT ARCHITECTURE SO INTERESTING."

— *Arthur Fleming to Hardie Phillip, July 10, 1925*

T he first project after Goodhue's death was a much needed heating plant completed in 1925 northeast of Throop Hall. This plain, industrial structure with exposed piers and a design of interlocking gears over a rear service door provided heated steam for the entire campus. Part of the structure served as an engineering laboratory for teaching purposes. In 1967 a newer plant south of California Boulevard was built. The original Steam Plant and Chemical Engineering Laboratory became a catch-all storage shed until it was demolished in 1996 to make way for the Fairchild Library of Engineering.

As the Steam Plant was being constructed Goodhue Associates began work on plans for an annex building to be connected to

These interlocking gears were located above a service door of the Steam Plant and Chemical Engineering Laboratory designed by the Goodhue Associates in 1925.

South view of Gates
Annex and Gates
Laboratory of Chemistry.
The annex was kept low
to maximize visibility of
the proposed Memorial
Building. Additional
arcades would be added to
those already attached to
Gates Laboratory.

Gates Laboratory of Chemistry. Similar to
the physics annex bordering Goodhue's central court on the south side, chemistry's new
wing on the north side would be kept low to
maximize visibility of the proposed domed
central structure. The wing would house a
library, a classroom, laboratories and offices,
and in the basement a large lecture room
and small seminar room. Funding would be
provided by Peter and Charles Gates who
gave the money for the first chemistry building. The plans were started in 1925 and the
building was completed in 1927. The materials used were reinforced concrete with a
stucco exterior making the building more
earthquake resistant than the hollow tile of
Gates Laboratory which cracked disastrously
in the 1971 Sylmar quake.

Fleming, who was Chairman of the
Board of Trustees, objected to Hardie
Phillip's initial design of the library's exteri-
or. He complained that the north facade
looked like a power plant with pilasters similar to those on the High Voltage and Steam

Plant buildings. Fleming suggested that
Clarence Stein, a former member of
Goodhue's firm and his assistant for the
Panama-California Exposition buildings in
San Diego, be called in as a consultant. After
seeing Stein's new plan for the library Noyes
told Hale, "[We have] got a real architect on
the job now and he will give us something
choice and unusual."

Stein's design amply fulfilled those pre-
dictions. Following Goodhue's philosophy of
taking inspirations wherever he found them,
(*je prends mon bien là où je le trouve*) Stein took
ideas from Byzantine architecture for the
vestibule which provides a transition to the
campus. A dome decorated with rings of
gold tiles, the names of the donors, and
circular stained glass skylights containing
stylized snowflakes defines the hallway. Two
sets of double doors, the outer ones of paneled wood with carved flowers, grape clus-
ters and scallops, and the inner ones of
brass-buttoned leather, open into a highly
decorative library. The rectangular room is

Opposite: Gates Annex
library. Interior hallway
dome decorated with rings
of gold tiles, the names of
donors, and circular
stained glass skylights
containing stylized
snowflakes.

Gates Annex library has
full-length windows cov-
ered by teakwood grilles
and framed by cast stone
lintels and columns.

lined with floor to ceiling bookshelves, each section divided by lathe-turned wooden uprights. The ceiling has molded concrete beams featuring colorful stencils of American-Indian designs and chemical symbols.

Noyes had suggested a patio, so Stein created full-length library windows opening onto a paved terrace with steps leading down to the garden. Goodhue and Stein's use of Mayan motifs for the interior of the principal San Diego Exposition building had started a Mayan Revival movement. At Caltech, Stein's library windows are covered by Spanish-inspired turned teakwood grilles, but the stone lintels and columns framing the windows are adorned with characters, animals and abstract motifs reminiscent of Mayan temples.

In order to provide daylight for Noyes "color experiment" demonstrations in the basement lecture hall, the room was extended several feet to the north of the library with pavement lights set into the tiled surface of the library's patio. In addition to its special illumination, the room was enriched with decorative beams. Many years later it was redone in a modern style and named the "Linus Pauling Lecture Hall" in recognition of the world famous chemist who taught freshman chemistry there.

A seminar room, adjacent to the lecture hall, retains its original atmosphere termed "Bohemian" by Fleming. Decorated cast concrete beams separate the vaults of the ceiling; tiled steps and a wrought iron balustrade lead down to a terra-cotta floor enlivened with small insets of black-bordered green, yellow and blue tiles. A water fountain, stair risers and corridor bases covered with glazed tiles in intricate floral designs complete the Spanish theme and make this an especially charming building.

By the 1930s, Noyes, who had become the country's leader in physical chemistry, wanted to expand his division to include organic chemistry and biochemistry. Charles Gates, who had already shared the cost of the first two buildings, persuaded his friends Edward and Amy Crellin to fund the final structure of the chemistry complex.

Edward W. Crellin, a civil engineer by training, had founded the Pittsburgh and Des Moines Steel Company. He was a member of the Caltech Associates, an Institute support group, and knew Professor Noyes well. Plans for the unit were drawn by the Goodhue Associates in 1931. However, bids exceeded the budget, and construction was put on hold.

Research groups, led by Linus Pauling, who received the 1954 Nobel Prize in Chemistry for his work on the nature of the chemical bond, desperately needed the laboratory space promised in Crellin. Hale came to the rescue by suggesting that unused space in Robinson Astrophysics could be made available for overflows from chemistry and physics.

Construction was resumed in 1937, and the Crellin building was occupied by April of 1938. Interior flexibility was the key. Fully-fitted laboratories and classsrooms could be altered according to changing requirements, and corridors on all levels connected through to the other chemistry buildings.

The design follows the basic form of the first chemistry laboratory, but the Churrigueresque decoration accenting the west entrance off San Pasqual Street is less florid than that around the main doorway of Gates Laboratory.

Another example of a drinking fountain set in colorful tile. Similar fountains can be found in Spain and the old cities of Morocco.

South entrance to Crellin Laboratory. This door, which would have opened toward the Memorial Building, was marked by a medallion over the door showing volumetric and Erlenmeyer flasks and a Bunsen burner. After the completion of Millikan Library the arcades were extended across this doorway forcing the demolition of the medallion and its chemistry symbols.

Aeronautics

"THE CALTECH WIND TUNNELS HELPED SOLVE DESIGN PROBLEMS FOR MORE THAN 600 TYPES OF
AIRCRAFT, INCLUDING VIRTUALLY ALL OF AMERICA'S MILITARY AIRCRAFT AND SEVERAL MILITARY MISSILES IN
WORLD WAR II."

— *Engineering and Science, January 1966*

In spite of the Wright brothers' early 1900s breakthrough in building flying machines, the United States lagged far behind Europe in furthering the new science of aeronautics. In 1926, when Daniel Guggenheim assigned 2.5 million dollars for the establishment of aeronautical schools in America, Millikan saw an opportunity to link Caltech with California's growing aircraft industry. He obtained $350,000 for the construction of a laboratory, and the establishment and operation of a Graduate School of Aeronautics.

Guggenheim Laboratory was designed by the Goodhue Associates. Its location behind Throop Hall, where Goodhue had planned a group of engineering buildings on either side of the east-west axis, serves as a transition between the academic and residential areas of the campus. Excavation began in 1927 and the building was in use the following year.

Although the laboratory was probably considered one of Caltech's least architecturally significant buildings, it soon became the center of important developments in aeronautics. The rectangular reinforced concrete building consists of three floors and two basements. The main feature and core of the interior was a ten-foot wind tunnel. Large enough to accommodate a "bigrig" truck, this giant rectangular doughnut with its redwood testing section became a vital experimental tool for testing scale models of airplanes. Equal access was given to Caltech's graduate students and aircraft companies such as Douglas, Northrop, Consolidated, Lockheed and Boeing. Support facilities consisted of an observation room, a wood shop, machine shop, balance room, offices, laboratories and a library. The basement contained more equipment to operate the wind tunnel and additional laboratories. In the sub-basement a water channel was used for research on sea-plane hulls, torpedoes and other water devices.

During a visit to Caltech in 1926, Theodore von Kármán, head of the Aerodynamics Institute at the Technical University of Aachen, increased the energy factor of the wind tunnel by redesigning it to use a closed-air circulation system.

Clark Blanchard Millikan, Robert Millikan's son, with a model of a DC-1 in Guggenheim Laboratory's 200-miles-per-hour, ten-foot wind tunnel. The tunnel became an important experimental tool for testing scale models of airplanes during World War II.

Unhappy with developments in Germany, he moved permanently to Caltech, and in 1930 was appointed professor and director of the newly formed Guggenheim Aeronautics Laboratory California Institute of Technology (GALCIT).

During World War II, GALCIT helped southern California become "the aircraft capital of the world" as industries, hurrying to supply the military, tested fighter planes and bombers in Caltech's wind tunnel. After the war, most aircraft companies built their own wind tunnels, some based on Caltech's design. GALCIT updated its facilities and continued to interact with industry by testing the effect of winds on cars, bridges,

buildings, stadiums and even athletes.

In 1987 the Whittier Narrows earthquake damaged the hypersensitive measuring equipment. This marked the end of the wind tunnel's life, and in 1997 it was demolished to make way for a smaller, high-tech model and new laboratories.

The Guggenheim Laboratory also witnessed the beginning of research in rocket propulsion, which led to the formation of the Jet Propulsion Laboratory in 1944. As early as 1935 scientists were assembling rockets in the laboratory, but their actual experiments took place in the Arroyo Seco, a dry river gorge near the western edge of Pasadena.

Over Guggenheim's rear service door is a carving of a propeller connected to oversize feathered wings poised between clouds and wave-washed mountains.

The sculpture illustrates how the art of flying progressed from a bird's flapping wings to the rotating propeller of a flying machine.

Entryway to the Guggenheim Laboratory. Topping the pilasters on either side of the door are sea planes flying beneath upside-down "Vs" representing mountains. According to Gerald Landry, Manager of the GALCIT Subsonic Wind Tunnels, the sea planes may have been modeled on the Douglas World Cruiser. In 1924 two planes, made by the Douglas company and owned by the United States Army Air Service, started from Clover Field in Santa Monica and took 175 days to complete a 29,000 mile round-the-world flight. For refueling or emergencies the planes were fitted with interchangeable landing gear of pontoons and wheels.

The exterior features of the Guggenheim building give only a hint of the work and intense activity that takes place inside. The monotony of the rectilinear form is relieved by splayed chamfered corners at the top, and decorative panels separating the windows on the first and second floors. Subtle designs relating to aviation focus attention on the main entry doors on the north side and a service door on the south side.

CHAPTER TEN

Humanities

"IT MUST BE ONE OF THE FINEST ARCHITECTURAL AND DECORATIVE FEATURES ON THE CAMPUS."

— *Noyes to Hale, 1926*

Dabney Hall of the Humanities. The south facade is similar to pueblo architecture of the southwest.

Although Amos Throop's philosophy of education focused on practical training, he also believed in the importance of the humanities. Hale, Millikan and Noyes agreed unequivocally that "through a fundamental training in the mathematical sciences and in history and literature there is provided the best possible preparation for life and leadership in this scientific age upon which we are now well embarked." William B. Munro, who was chosen to head the Division of Humanities, said that "scientific erudition can be illuminated by humanism, and technical skill vivified by imagination."

On June 8, 1926, Noyes had written to Hale suggesting an immediate campaign to raise money for a building. "A Hall of the Humanities will be a unique feature in a scientific school, and will do much to

Dabney Hall of the Humanities, west facade. This rendering by James Perry Wilson shows the original design of the building. Panels of colored tile in a geometric pattern were to fill the spaces between the windows and spell out the names of the donors in a horizontal band below the third floor windows. Wilson was a valued member of Goodhue's architectural staff. Goodhue referred to him as "the office sciographer" meaning a "caster of shadows."

North Elevation of Dabney Hall of the Humanities. Architect's drawing shows an ornamental panel of small colored tiles spaced at intervals in the stucco.

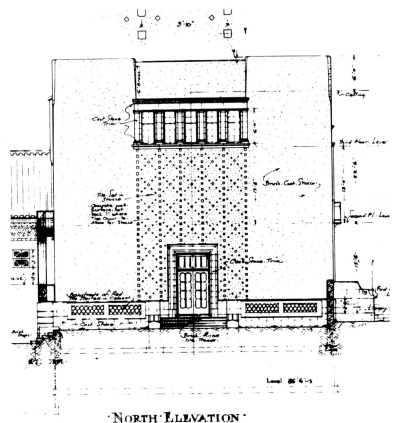

· NORTH·ELEVATION ·

Right: Dabney Garden fountain. The backdrop has similar tile work to that planned for the north facade.

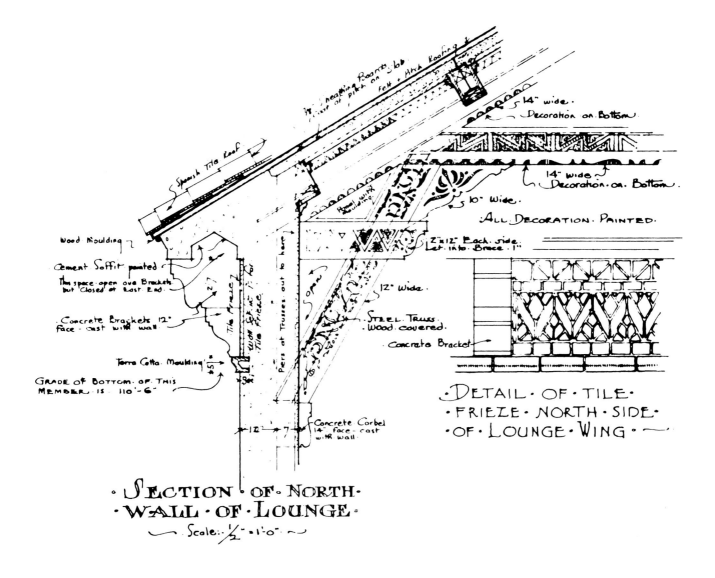

Wood Moulding

Cement Soffit painted

This space open over Brackets but closed at last end.

Concrete Brackets 12" face - cast with wall

Terra Cotta Moulding

GRADE OF BOTTOM. OF THIS MEMBER IS 110'-6"

Spanish Tile Roof

Sheathing Boards bb Coat of pitch on 1 felt Mtrd Roofing

Piers at Trusses out to here

The Frieze

Wood Frame 1" for Tile Frieze

Concrete Corbel 14" face - cast with wall

STEEL TRUSS. WOOD covered.

Concrete Bracket

12" Wide.

2"x12" Each side. Let into Brace 1"

Open

14" wide. Decoration on Bottom.

14" wide. Decoration on Bottom.

10" Wide.

ALL DECORATION PAINTED.

·SECTION· OF· NORTH·
·WALL· OF· LOUNGE·
Scale: ½" = 1'-0"

·DETAIL· OF· TILE·
·FRIEZE· NORTH· SIDE·
·OF· LOUNGE· WING· ~

North Wall of Dabney lounge. Architect's drawing of tile work planned for the cornice area above the French doors of the lounge.

overcome the impression that we are a narrow technical school." He stressed that the cost should not be less than $200,000 "for it must be one of the finest architectural and decorative features on the campus." According to a report *California Institute in 1928* "classes in literature, history and philosophy have had to be conducted in physics and chemistry laboratories amid switchboards and test-tube racks and a varied assortment of distracting sounds and smells."

Mr. and Mrs. Joseph B. Dabney gave $250,000 for the construction and furnishings of the building. Joseph Dabney was born on a farm in Iowa. Although he trained as a lawyer, he found his vocation as a pio-

neer in California's oil development. The hall was designed by the Goodhue Associates with Clarence Stein as consultant. Drawings were executed in August, 1927, construction completed by the end of 1928, and the building officially opened in March, 1929.

Dabney Hall of the Humanities sits parallel to Gates Laboratory of Chemistry and forms the north-east corner of Goodhue's central court. The main section has three stories and a basement. A one-story wing with a Spanish-tiled roof houses a lounge. A charming walled garden is bordered on two sides by the "L" shape of the building.

Treasure Room in
Dabney Hall. Cast iron
work featuring abstract
motifs frames the door to
the paneled Treasure
Room. Once used for
exhibits, this room has
now been divided into
offices for Development.

Dabney Hall wing furnished as a student lounge. A highbacked bench on the south wall (partially hidden by the lampshade) was created by Pasadena cabinetmaker George S. Hunt. The back panel features a carving of the proposed domed Memorial Building and reflecting pool, bordered by the cypress trees and the West Court academic buildings. This bench is now located in the first floor corridor.

Originally the first floor consisted of a library with a spiral staircase to basement stacks, a treasure room, and administrative offices. On the second floor was a large lecture room above the library, and smaller classrooms with more seminar rooms on the third floor. Some of the third floor offices opened onto a loggia with a view of the mountains in the distance, and the garden below. Rooms for student clubs were located in the basement. As the Institute's needs have changed the interior rooms have been re-arranged. Most of the humanities division has moved to Baxter Hall, and the vacated space is being used by offices for Development.

Hale did his best to retain the Churrigueresque and Moorish elements which he felt expressed the Spanish theme of the master plan. But the inheritors of Goodhue's legacy took advantage of Dabney Hall's location away from the planned central building with its elaborate Spanish frontispiece, to show off their master's latest work. The building is an example of Goodhue's use of abstract ornamentation which foreshadowed the art deco movement.

The exterior of Dabney Hall, especially the south facade, gives an impression of pueblo architecture with rounded edges at the roof line, and diagonally-cut corners creating an effect of inward-sloping walls.

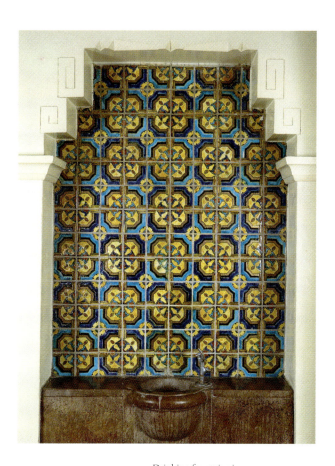

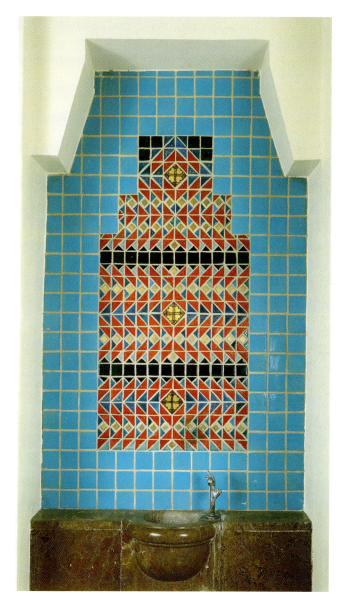

Drinking fountains in
Dabney Hall. A leaf motif
forms the back drop of a
first floor fountain. A basement level fountain is
enhanced by a chevron
design of red, yellow and
black tiles on a blue background. Similar colors
might have been used for
the exterior tile work of
the building.

Dabney Hall, west entry door. Designs in the wrought iron gates recall Mayan motifs. The squared spiral at the top is the symbol for Kulkulcán, wind god of vegetation and rain, called Quetzalcoatl by the Aztecs. The spiral design is found on ruins at Chichen Itzá and El Tajún.

Originally the designers had planned to relieve the monotony of the building's plain tan walls with decorative tile work in a variety of forms. On the west facade, the proposed panels of colored tile in a geometric pattern between the windows were replaced with a cast-stone diamond-shaped diaper design. Tile work spelling out the names of the donors was to form a horizontal molding below the third floor windows. A pattern of tiles was to decorate the stucco around the north entrance. The walls of niches housing benches at the north and south ends of the loggia were to have been decorated with bright yellow Tunis tiles in a green border.

The final cost of the building came to $213,933.89 so there should have been sufficient money for the tile work and the

interior furnishings. But Hale seems to have doubted Stein's ability with tile, "Stein is much better than Phillip...though I don't trust him with tiles." In addition, the members of the Building Committee may have hesitated to introduce such a different feature on an important building.

Fortunately, many of the planned interior elements were installed. In order to retain continuity between the buildings, the main corridor has a padre tile floor, a groined vaulted ceiling with wavy plaster and wrought-iron doors and light fixtures. Iron gates with abstract shapes influenced by Mayan designs frame the west entrance, the original doorway to the humanities library and a space designated as the Treasure Room. Decorative tile work with a leaf motif backs a water fountain set in a marble basin.

Noyes had stipulated that the large lounge in the wing of Dabney Hall was to be used for cultural and social functions of an academic nature, such as lectures, faculty meetings, afternoon teas or simple buffet suppers. More raucous events such as student dances should be held in Culbertson Hall. To create an elegant atmosphere, the lounge was designed with a wide planked oak floor, a high beamed ceiling, half-paneled walls, light fixtures decorated with colorful zigzag designs and full-length French doors made of teak opening onto the garden.

After the building was completed the exterior portales of Gates were extended along the south side of Dabney Hall, leaving a small court to protect an especially large and old Engelmann oak tree. Niches, featuring a backdrop of blue, yellow and white tiles, were placed where the arcades abut each building.

Astrophysics

"The design of our Astrophysical Lab, with its two sub-basements, pit 75' deep, tower for coelostat telescope, two domes, 'solar furnace' and other special features, illustrates the importance of adapting a building for the requirements of the men who work in it."

— *Hale to Morgan, August 12, 1929*

From his early days dabbling in instruments and looking at outer space, Hale sought to build larger and better telescopes. Although ill health forced him to resign as director of the Mount Wilson Observatory in 1923, he continued to pursue his ambition to build a 200-inch telescope. In 1928, the International Education Board of the Rockefeller Foundation approved Hale's $6 million request. To the bitter disappointment of the Carnegie Foundation, which ran the Mount Wilson Observatory, the IEB stipulated that the telescope should be built and operated by an educational organization.

Caltech was the obvious choice. The honor of building the world's largest telescope added an exciting dimension to the growth of the Institute. An Observatory Council, chaired by Hale, was formed to plan, build and operate the project. An endowment, provided by Henry Robinson, financed the administrative costs of the observatory and the Astrophysics Laboratory which was then named in his honor.

Henry W. Robinson had become a trustee of Throop Polytechnic in 1907. A lawyer by training, Robinson's many business interests included telephone companies, electrical power, railways and banking. Hale spoke of his "unparalleled generosity" toward Caltech. As well as underwriting the

Russell Porter at his drawing board. He executed beautiful sketches for the campus astrophysics buildings and was responsible for designing the Observatory on Mount Palomar.

operation of the astrophysics program, he
founded, in 1926, a support group for the
Institute known as the California Institute
Associates, set up an endowment fund for
the humanities division, and provided
money for a geology building.

Plans called for a complex of three buildings on the Caltech campus: an Optical Shop
for polishing the mirror; a Machine Shop;
and an Astrophysics Laboratory to serve as
the Pasadena headquarters of the
Observatory staff and of the Graduate

The Machine Shop's south
wall featured a running
"v" design below the soft-
ened roof line and a dia-
per design that matched
the Optical Shop around
the frames of the front
and side doors.

Right: The Optical Shop
had an interlocking dia-
mond-shaped pattern on
the north and south
facade. An arch known as
Porter's arch joined the
two shops. The 200" mir-
ror had to be maneuvered
through this arch before
and after being polished in
the Optical Shop.

School of Astrophysics. The Goodhue Associates were hired to design the campus buildings but architect Gustave Iser executed the drawings for the shops. Hale chose Russell Porter to work with the architects on campus, and to be solely responsible for the Observatory and its support buildings. After using small telescopes to test various sites, Porter recommended Palomar Mountain, 160 miles southeast of Pasadena as the best location.

Russell W. Porter was born in 1871 in Vermont. Prior to his interest in astronomy,

Porter's early career included studies at MIT in civil engineering and architecture, painting classes, six trips to the Arctic, farming, home construction and teaching architecture. A natural artist and superb draftsman who drew perfect parallel lines without a tool, Porter brought creativity and precision to the telescope project. In 1928, at the age of 57, he was hired on a temporary basis for a few months and stayed for two decades.

Although Hale was frequently at odds with the Goodhue Associates, Porter developed a good working relationship with

them. Adept at sketching he drew several designs for the Optical Shop, some with elaborate towers and an abundance of diaper decoration. Confined by financial limitations and Hale's advice that "simplicity seems...in keeping with the uses of the buildings which will be bare and unfinished within...plus the work is dirty," the final design was a 57 foot-high rectangular building with exposed pylons similar to the High Voltage Laboratory.

The Machine Shop, where the instruments for the telescope were made, was a long one-story building attached to its sister building, the Optical Shop, by a gracious rounded arch beneath a bridge. Known as Porter's arch, it became an important part of the telescope project. In 1936, after its long journey from the Corning Glass Works, the 200-inch mirror was gently steered through the arch for its years of grinding and polishing in the Optical Shop. In 1947, after an interruption for World War II specialized projects, the mirror was finally finished and moved to Palomar. The Machine Shop was torn down in 1969 to be replaced by the

Downs-Lauritsen Physics building, but the
Optical Shop was used for the construction
of the synchrotron for Nuclear Physics.
After the removal of the synchrotron in
1970, the space housed reflectors for radio
telescopes. Since then, part of the interior
has been divided into offices for physics
faculty.

Porter referred to Robinson Astrophysics
as the "gem of the Institute group." The
reinforced concrete building has two floors
above ground, one basement, two sub-basements and a rectangular well containing a

Porter's rendering of the
Machine Shop and arch
with Guggenheim
Laboratory of Aeronautics
in the background.

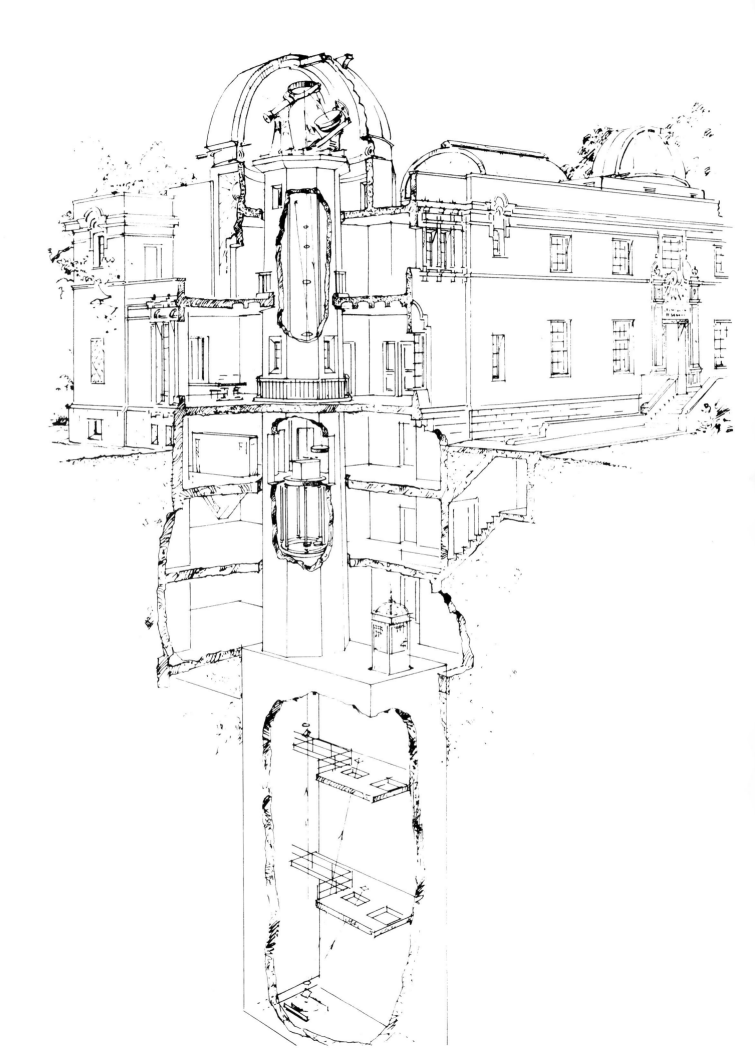

Left: Cutaway drawing of Robinson Laboratory of Astrophysics. The rectangular well is 75' deep and contains the spectrograph and other instruments.

200" disk being ground and polished in the Optical Shop.

ASTROPHYSICS LABORATORY ⚬ CAL·INSTITUTE OF TECHNOLOGY

Porter's rendering of
Robinson Astrophysics.

75-foot spectrograph and other instruments.
An observation dome on the roof was built
as a 1:10 scale model of the 200-inch telescope to test many of its design features.
This dome and a photographic telescope are
now used to train students.

Cast stone carvings enhance the architecture and reflect the purpose of the laboratory. Sun rays on the wall below the dome and
over the main entrance announce the study
of solar astronomy. Light fixtures representing observatory models on either side of the
doorway were originally designed by Porter
for the Machine Shop, but were considered
too elaborate. The light fixture inside the
vestibule represents an armillary sphere,

Robinson Astrophysics
with observation dome
and a carving of the sun
to announce the study of
solar astronomy.

Rendering and photographs of main entrance to Robinson Astrophysics.

Detail of Robinson
Astrophysics library. The
beamed ceiling, by A. T.
Heinsbergen & Company,
is decorated with stencil
work that incorporates
Greek symbols of the
zodiacal constellations. A
pendant light fixture features Roman symbols.

Light fixtures on either side of the main entrance to Robinson Astrophysics are observatory models. Their glass has turned purple because of sunlight reacting with the manganese dioxide mixed in the sand during the manufacturing process.

"an old astronomical instrument composed of rings representing the positions of important circles of the celestial sphere." Light fixtures in the corridors are decorated with Saturn and its rings, and three dimensional stars.

Hale wanted the astrophysics library to conform to the Spanish theme of the campus and have a similar design to the chemistry library. Located at the south end of the first floor the space is organized around the octagonal-shaped tower of the coelostat telescope. Wooden bookshelves in a Spanish style line the walls. Cork flooring, oak reading tables, leather chairs, and portraits of famous astronomers complete the Spanish-academic ambiance.

Having been chosen to build Hale's dream telescope in 1928, Caltech's astrophysics research is now supplemented by an exceptional group of observatories: the Palomar Observatory which houses the Hale 200-inch telescope, the Owens Valley Radio Observatory, and the Caltech

Submillimeter Observatory on Mauna Kea, Hawaii. In addition, the Institute and the University of California jointly operate the W. M. Keck Observatory on Mauna Kea. Caltech's former solar observatory at Big Bear has been purchased by the New Jersey Institute of Technology.

Drinking fountain in the corridor of Robinson Astrophysics.

CHAPTER TWELVE

Biology and Geology

"It [Biology] is not just an individual building, but a very definite part of the whole group. It will dictate the design, grouping, spacing, etc. of the buildings on its side of the lagoon, and also tie up the building on the other side."

— *Hardie Phillip to Morgan, September 12, 1927*

Biology

As illustrated in Goodhue's color rendering of his master plan, the West Court was to form a major approach to the Memorial Building and the main plaza of the campus. A long reflecting pool would define the court's axis, with two biology buildings forming the north edge and two geology buildings and an auditorium the south. Continuous arcades connected to the buildings would terminate in domed porches, miniature versions of the tiled dome of the centerpiece.

On several occasions Hale stressed the importance of this area. In a letter to Fleming dated October 28, 1927 he wrote, "This domed building establishes the keynote of our entire scheme, and it cannot be ignored in designing the other buildings. While we have accepted certain deviations from this style in buildings not closely tied to this central feature, we certainly cannot do so in the axial group flanking the long pools."

Now that the Institute had established a strong program in the physical sciences Noyes, who had begun research work on the newly discovered hormone insulin, urged an expansion into biochemistry and biophysics. He felt that courses in biology were essential to the all-encompassing education designed by Caltech for its students in engineering and science. Millikan, on the other hand was more ambitious. In 1925 he proposed a pre-medical program or even a medical school, but Hale considered this to be beyond Caltech's administrative scope. In keeping with a basic science curriculum, a biology division was added.

Thomas Hunt Morgan, a biologist at Columbia University, was the unanimous choice to chair the new division. Morgan was born in 1866 to a well-known southern family in Lexington, Kentucky. Although his research encompassed a large variety of plants and animals, Morgan became famous for his work on fruit flies, establishing the chromosome theory of heredity which revolutionized genetic research. He received a Nobel Prize in 1933.

Morgan was eager to come to Caltech because it would give him the opportunity to establish, on his own terms, a division

Thomas Hunt Morgan. He received the 1933 Nobel Prize in Physiology or Medicine, and was the first chairman of Caltech's biology division.

which would differ from the traditional academic combination of zoology and botany. It would be the first biology department not associated with a medical school. However, he wanted assurances of a building and an $80,000 annual budget.

Initially two three-story buildings were planned with a quadrangle extension at the northwest corner to be added later. The drawings and design would be executed by the Goodhue Associates and Clarence Stein. The estimated cost was $4 million.

Even though Morgan had been hired and the architects had begun work on the drawings, there was confusion over raising the

money. Caltech's Board of Trustees was made up of influential and wealthy entrepreneurs. Trustees Allan C. Balch and William George Kerckhoff, with three other partners, owned utility companies which prospered with the influx of new residents into southern California and the booming economy of the 1920s. Fleming, who was President of the Board, mistakenly thought that Balch had agreed to provide $2 million when in fact he had only promised $1 million. Eventually the Rockefeller-funded General Education Board provided $2 million, Caltech raised another $1 million and Balch persuaded his friend and partner, William

Kerckhoff I's west facade features Churrigueresque volutes, fruit vines, and bands of eight-pointed stars with an abundance of animals, fish and plants. A chain of monkeys, crabs, lobsters, octopi, corn, peapods and seahorses enliven the facade.

Kerckhoff I and II, south facade circa 1930. In the style of Moorish architecture, a long expanse of plain wall was broken by ornamented stairwell towers and windows.

Kerckhoff I and II, south facade circa 1985. In 1981 the carefully pruned cypress trees, which had deteriorated, were replaced with climbing wisteria.

The Kerckhoff I tower displays abstract ornamentation with the fine, flatter details of the Plateresque. In contrast the Kerckhoff II tower is decorated with plants. Cacti and sunflowers are typical of the region, and corn and evening primrose were used in genetic research.

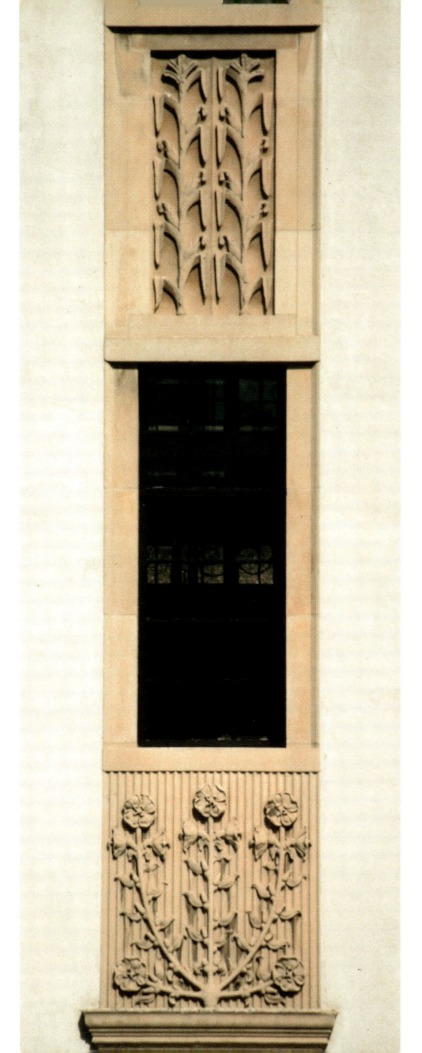

Kerckhoff, to give $1 million. Kerckhoff's gift, however, carried the proviso that the buildings be named for him. As Balch wished to remain anonymous and the other gifts carried no demands, Kerckhoff's name was used for both buildings.

More than any other division chairman, Morgan became deeply involved in every detail of his buildings from the location of rooms to the exact placement of electrical outlets. He believed in the importance of daylight for laboratory spaces, and wanted more light than would be provided by the half-windows of the basement level in the Goodhue Associates plan. After many discussions a compromise was reached. Because of the arcade border, the windows facing Goodhue's ceremonial courtyard would remain as planned but the ground level on the north side of the building would be lowered to permit taller windows. Although Morgan fussed over the light aspect, he was also sensitive to Hale's insistence on retaining the Spanish theme of Goodhue's master plan. For instance, he suggested centering a second floor window over a doorway on the west facade to accommodate the cast stone work planned to reflect the Churrigueresque decoration around the main entrance and windows of the Memorial Building.

The architects, backed by Fleming, wanted both biology buildings built at the same time. Fleming's reason was to save money on the construction, and the architects reason was to establish the overall plan of the west court.

Morgan, already slow at stating his requirements for the first building to be devoted to his own work (genetics and embryology), kept stalling on the second building (physiology). He felt unable to devise a layout until he had hired his faculty

CHEMISTRY GROUP · THIRD UNIT   BIOLOGY GROUP · SECOND UNIT

CALIFORNIA INSTITUTE OF TECHNOLOGY · PASADENA · CALIFORNIA · VIEW FROM SAN PASQUAL STREET   MAYERS · MURRAY · & PHILLIP · ARCHITECTS

Artist's rendering of Kerckhoff II and Crellin building with proposed domed building behind.

On either side of the library window is a scallop-edged carving containing a squid and an octopus, both sitting beneath stylized kelp supporting a star fish.

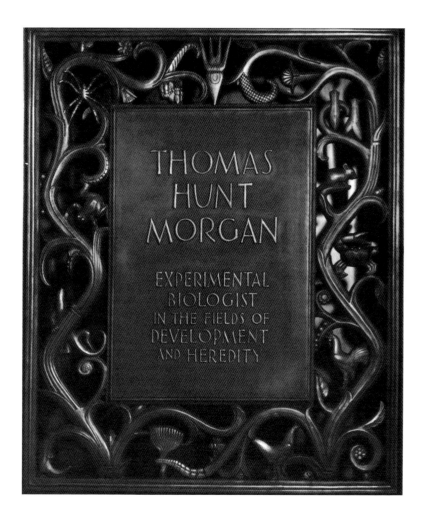

Biology Library. In 1951, a small bookcase and bronze plaque dedicated to Morgan, who had died in 1945, were installed on the library's east wall. The designer, Dr. Albert Stewart of Scripps College, incorporated into the grillwork frame the various plants and animals with which the famous biologist worked.

and understood their needs. This situation combined with the confusion over funding, influenced Millikan's decision to proceed only with the construction of Kerckhoff I. Ground was broken in 1927 and construction completed soon after Morgan's arrival in Pasadena in the summer of 1928.

Architectural eclecticism came into vogue between the two world wars. Architects like Bertram Goodhue, recognizing the importance of precedent, took forms and motifs from many different sources, simplifying and assembling them in new ways. Art historian Helen Searing commented, "strict imitation...was not the aim...and ornament was often freely invented to speak immediately of each building's purpose." In his earlier ecclesiastical work on the east coast Goodhue had used Gothic architecture

as his inspiration. In the same way as carvings on the cathedrals in Europe served as history books of the period and recounted the stories of the Bible, cast stone carvings at Caltech could be used to express the purpose of the building. Most of the exterior ornamentation on the Kerckhoff buildings represents various aspects of research in biology.

The west facade of Kerckhoff I facing Wilson features an abundance of animals, fish and plants. As part of the approach to the grand central building, the continuous south facade facing the proposed reflecting pools has a long expanse of plain wall broken by ornamentated stairwell towers and windows. Crabs form the keystones of the windows and plants used in genetic research decorate a tower.

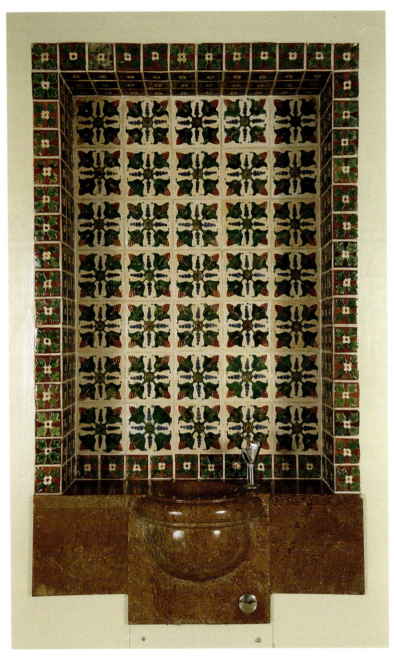

To avoid the noise of the general traffic areas, Morgan located the biology library as a north-facing wing on the second floor of Kerckhoff II. On each side of the wing, windows with exterior frames of turned teak, overlook a garden. Carvings depicting sea life surround the main window. Because libraries were revered as the source of knowledge, the two-story biology reading room, furnished with wooden bookcases, rectangular reading tables and leather chairs, is elegant and serene. Hexagonal-shaped light fixtures featuring stylized squid, sea horses and radiolarians hang from a coffered teak ceiling.

The first floor corridors retain the Spanish features of other Goodhue buildings including water fountains richly decorated with Persian tiles and verde marble.

A fiddler crab, whose long bow is used in courting and defense, sits above an archway on the east side of Kerckhoff II.

GEOLOGY

"SOUTHERN CALIFORNIA IS A REGION ALMOST UNRIVALED FOR GEOLOGIC INVESTIGATION."

— *Caltech Bulletin, 1925*

In announcing the establishment of a Department of Geology in 1925, the Caltech Bulletin emphasized the abundance and variety of geological structures within easy reach of Pasadena. "The region likewise offers excellent opportunity for studies in physical and geological seismology...in different phases of paleontology, and in other branches of geology." Moreover, "field work in any of these lines can be carried on comfortably throughout the entire year."

Dr. John P. Buwalda, who had held professorships in geology at Yale and Berkeley, was hired to run the department. Buwalda came to Caltech in 1925 with the understanding that a building would materialize eventually, but until money was available geology would share space with physics in the West Bridge building.

Seeley W. Mudd Laboratory of the Geological Sciences (North Mudd). Hale agreed to Phillip's idea to move the auditorium farther south so that geology could have more space. This 1930 rendering by James Perry Wilson shows that the auditorium would share an entrance through the connected laboratory building.

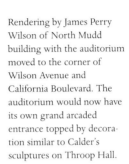

Rendering by James Perry Wilson of North Mudd building with the auditorium moved to the corner of Wilson Avenue and California Boulevard. The auditorium would now have its own grand arcaded entrance topped by decoration similar to Calder's sculptures on Throop Hall.

At the same time, a Seismological Research Laboratory, funded by the Carnegie Institution, was built in the San Rafael district west of the Arroyo Seco. The administration of the program was shared by Carnegie and Caltech until 1937 when seismology became part of the Division of Geological Sciences.

By 1928 geology had outgrown its temporary home and paleontology desperately needed exhibit space. In fact, the geology division now needed the same amount of space as biology.

Hardie Phillip, representing the Goodhue Associates, suggested that the auditorium, which took up a section of the West Court opposite Kerchoff I, could be moved farther to the south. He felt that extending geology and paleontology all the way to Wilson Avenue symmetrical to biology was "perfectly feasible...and it sacrificed nothing essential of the original Goodhue scheme." Hale concurred and the change was approved by the Executive Council in October, 1929.

Funds for the two buildings were being provided by the Mudd and Robinson families. Mrs. Seeley W. Mudd had agreed to underwrite a geology building in memory of her husband. Born in St. Louis in 1861, Seeley Wintersmith Mudd was "recognized as one of the most successful mining engineers of his time." Trustee Henry M. Robinson and his wife Laurabelle funded the second geology building named in honor of Laurabelle's father, Charles Arms, who had widespread mining interests in gold and silver.

To save on construction costs, the Institute decided to proceed with the second biology building (Kerckhoff II), the two geology buildings (Arms and Mudd now North Mudd), and the third section of the chemistry complex (Crellin) all at one time. By April, 1931, work was proceeding on the drawings, the contractor had started excavation, costs were being assembled, and Phillip had agreed to come to Pasadena to supervise the project.

At a meeting of the Executive Council on December 2, 1931 it was learned that the costs for Crellin and Kerckhoff II were greatly in excess of funds available. The country was in the midst of the Great Depression and much of Caltech's money and that of its donors was tied up in the rapidly falling stock market. Hale opined that "under circumstances existing at present, it is inadvisable to construct new buildings of any kind unless there is urgent necessity for so doing." It was agreed that all available funds were needed for the immediate running of the Institute. The geology donors concurred. The motion stated, "erection of the Chemistry, Biology, and both Geology buildings be indefinitely deferred."

The administration anticipated only a short delay, but it was six years before the building program could be continued.

Meanwhile the cypress trees, which had been planted on either side of the courtyard after the completion of Kerckhoff I, stood like lost sentinels waiting for the buildings and arcades which they were destined to guard.

Construction resumed in 1937. Chemistry was completed in the same year, and biology and the two geology buildings were occupied by the end of 1938. Funds were still tight and luxury items, such as stencil work on the ceilings of the paleontology museum and the geology library were eliminated.

Construction of the West Court was resumed in 1937 after a six-year delay caused by shortage of funds.

A marble bird bath, purchased in London, was given to the geology division in 1939 by Harvey S. Mudd, who was head of his father's mining business. In a letter of appreciation Buwalda wrote, "When you generously suggested presenting the attractively sculptured bird bath you commented, perhaps jokingly, that you were not certain whether it would fit best into the Court of the Oak or into your own garden... The birds bathe in it so frequently and throw water out so vigorously that the janitor has had to go to the custom of refilling it every morning."

First floor wing of Charles Arms Laboratory of the Geological Sciences, originally used as a paleontology museum.

With greater awareness of earthquakes, the structural plans for the geology buildings (three stories above ground and two basements) were revised to withstand the stresses of a major quake. The first floor of a rectangular wing extending to the south of the Arms building was originally designed as a paleontology museum. In 1959 the space was divided up into administrative offices. The south doorway, intended as a public entrance from California Boulevard to the museum, is decorated in the Churrigueresque style. Above the door is a medallion featuring the geological symbols of a pick and a hammer.

On the courtyard side, the buildings have plain walls with decoration concentrated on the stairwell towers, mirror images of the biology towers. The Arms tower shows Churrigueresque-style carvings in keeping with the building's south facing doorway. The designs on the tower of North Mudd mimic those on Kerckhoff I. Botany and paleontology are represented by plants and shells intricately woven into a Plateresque-style carving.

The west face of North Mudd balances the facade of Kerckhoff I in preparation for the grand approach to the proposed Memorial Building. As on the biology building, the Goodhue Associates deviated from the strictly Churrigueresque style by incorporating geological symbols into the cast stone carvings.

At the dedication of the geology buildings on March 14, 1939, Millikan said, "After years of being looked after and protected, and having its nose wiped and its eyes dried and its bib cleaned and its bed made by its older brother physics, geology has at last grown to man's estate and is today fully in command of its castle from which it now can issue forth well equipped and accoutered to go out on its own and conquer the earth, for that is just its job."

Hexagonal-shaped lamps featuring trilobites surround Arms Laboratory's south doorway.

Arms Laboratory's south doorway was the public entrance to the paleontology museum. It is decorated in the Churrigueresque style with a medallion showing the geological symbols of a pick and a hammer above the window.

North Mudd tower features a Plateresque style carving combining mofits from botany and paleontology. A fanciful snowflake sits like a crown above a lambrequin. A leafy vine twines around flower shapes symbolic of the basic forms of nature.

The pineapple-like pods and wavy leaves may belong to the poppy family because the Matilija poppy was adopted as Caltech's flower in 1916. A decorative cornice is interrupted by arched panels featuring a scallop shell set in a zigzag-bordered frame.

Right: Detail of North Mudd library window. The window is flanked by two columns of carvings depicting the traditional approach to teaching geology. The outside column represents historical geology with a carving of the tree of life. The roots of a tree, an amoeba, trilobite, ostracoderm, brontosaurus, stegosaurus, mammoth and a man on a horse show the progression of the species. The column next to the window contains pictures based on physical geology: pick and hammer, waterfall, volcano, columnar basalt, stalactites and stalagmites, and canyon country. Between the columns are crystal shapes symbolizing mineralogy.

Ocean, Mountains, Clouds. This small carving is located at the top of a wall above the arcades at the east end of North Mudd. According to ancient Greek philosophers Fire, Water, Earth and Air were the essential components of all matter. Today, earth scientists study air and water in the atmosphere (the clouds), earth and fire in geology (the mountains and volcanoes), and water in oceanography (the waves).

PART FOUR
Gordon
Kaufmann

CHAPTER THIRTEEN

The Athenaeum

"The purpose of the Athenaeum is to promote social intercourse among lovers of science, literature, and art, by creating a center of intellectual and social life, more particularly for persons connected with the Henry E. Huntington Library and Art Gallery, the Mount Wilson Observatory of the Carnegie Institution of Washington, and the California Institute of Technology."

— Athenaeum Handbook, 1931

The name Athenaeum comes from Athena, the Greek goddess of wisdom, who ruled all intellectual and practical aspects of civic life. Throughout history academies for the promotion of learning have assembled in buildings called Athenaeums. One of George Ellery Hale's many visions was a social gathering place for the great thinkers of Caltech and its associated institutions. Modeling his vision on London's Athenaeum founded in 1824 by Sir Walter Scott and Thomas Moore, Hale expected Caltech's members to be distinguished in science, literature, arts or public

Goodhue's 1925 rendering of the proposed Athenaeum showing an arcaded facade and curved driveway facing Hill Avenue.

The Athenaeum's east elevation as viewed from Hill Avenue.

Gordon Bernie Kaufman was the architect chosen to design the Athenaeum and Student Dormitories. He was a popular and prolific architect. Like Johnson, Coate, and Neff, his residential designs feature a blend of different Mediterranean influences.

service. A document in the Institute Archives explains why Caltech was considered an appropriate location. "There is in Southern California the nucleus of a group of men of intellectual power and achievement as comprehensive and important as exists perhaps in any center in this country." The document outlines the club's purpose: it should be a place for principal investigators in a variety of disciplines to discuss their work with each other as well as with graduate students; for academics to communicate with civic leaders; for staff to live; and for members of the community to spend leisure hours in a comfortable library or club room. Special dinners or regular gatherings could be held "to hear discussions on topics of interest in science and art, literature, history and government by those best prepared to tell of the fascinating developments in those fields."

Allan and Janet Balch provided the necessary funds which would bring Hale's dream to fruition. Allan Balch was born in Valley Falls, New York, in 1864. He graduated in

electrical engineering from Cornell University where he met his future wife. After moving to Los Angeles in 1896, he helped to pioneer the use of electric power for irrigation pumping and oil drilling. With partners Henry O'Melveny and William Kerckhoff, Balch became rich buying and selling companies which provided utilities for southern California. Having no children of their own, Allan and Janet Balch gave their money and time to educational and cultural causes in the Southland. Balch joined Caltech's Board of Trustees in 1925, serving as President from 1933 until his death in 1943. He was a founding member of The Caltech Associates, contributed $1 million towards Caltech's Biology complex, and established the Balch Graduate School of the Geological Sciences at Caltech.

In 1929 Balch transferred stocks and bonds to the Institute to fund its proposed Athenaeum. Fortunately, Caltech converted his gift into cash just before the stock market crashed. While the completion of the academic buildings at the west end of campus had to be put on hold because of lack of funds, the Institute had in its possession approximately $500,000 earmarked for a luxurious social center.

Goodhue's 1917 Block Plan for Throop College included a residential section at the east end of the campus. He told Hale in a letter dated June 5, 1923, that he was sending "some blue prints of a scheme that suddenly entered my head for the Dormitories and Dormitory section." He explained that he had located the Athenaeum Club according to Mr. Fleming's wishes but he would prefer "the other corner as being quieter and already quite beautifully wooded."

On March 30, 1925, a newspaper article stated that, "Designs have just been completed for the beautiful dormitories, dining halls, campanile and faculty club-house which will complement the group of academic buildings at the California Institute of Technology...The drawings were prepared

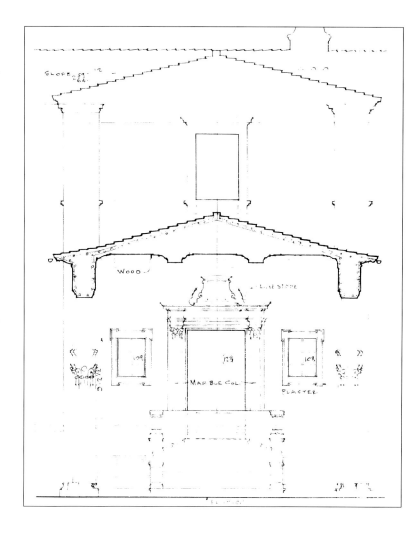

Architect's drawing of Athenaeum's south elevation and entryway.

SOUTH ELEVATION

from preliminary sketches by the late Bertram G. Goodhue, architect." The article explained that the plans had been tentatively approved by the Board of Trustees at a cost of $4 million. Goodhue's birds-eye illustration, showing buildings with a campanile at the far end, and a rendering of the proposed Athenaeum were included.

By 1928, the Goodhue Associates had completed several sections of the original plan and other buildings were in the design phase. However, Hale and the Board of Trustees were displeased with certain aspects of the arrangement. At a meeting of the Executive Council on February 21, 1928, the balance of the plan, which consisted of the central domed building, student dormitories and Athenaeum, was discussed. The question was raised whether the work "should be done by the Bertram G. Goodhue Associates and Clarence S. Stein, or whether the Institute should employ other architects for any part of it." A lengthy discussion spawned two committees: one to find a local architect for the dormitory group; the other to study the problems of student life.

On March 7 of the same year Hale wrote to Balch "I am convinced that a Southern California architect should be employed to design the Institute dormitories." He asked Balch to vote as his proxy in favor of architects Reginald Johnson, Gordon Kaufmann, Garrett Van Pelt, or John and David Allison. "I assume, of course, that Mr. Goodhue's

The Athenaeum's entrance hall is Greco-Roman with a travertine floor and fluted pilasters with triangular pediment framing a doorway. The hall's main feature, a vaulted ceiling, has trompe l'oeil coffers and rosettes.

The showpiece of the Athenaeum's main dining room is a magnificent beamed ceiling painted in a style called "grotesque," featuring medallions, cherubs and foliage. Kaufmann used painted ceilings in several of his projects after finding an Italian muralist and consummate artist in Giovanni Battista Smeraldi, who learned his trade at the Vatican before coming to the United States in 1889. Among his many masterpieces, Smeraldi contributed to the decoration of the Blue Room at the White House, the Grand Central Station in New York, and the Biltmore Hotel in Los Angeles.

complete design for the athaneum proper, which he worked out in all its details, will be used." At a meeting of the Board of Trustees a few days later (March 13), Noyes gave a report on the Athenaeum plan which contained the following points: (1) To be very attractive in architectural design and in interior decoration (as in the design of Bertram G. Goodhue); (2) To be located at the eastern end of the Institute campus; (3) To contain the rooms provided in the Goodhue design. The cost of the building "as designed by Mr. Goodhue would be approximately $350,000." Evidently the architect chosen to develop student housing would be expected to incorporate Goodhue's concept and plan in any design of the Athenaeum.

Architect Gordon Bernie Kaufmann was selected. Born in London in 1888, Kaufman's mother was Scottish and his father German. After training at the London Polytechnic and Royal College of Art, he served as an apprentice in an architect's office before emigrating to Canada. Hoping to improve his wife's delicate health, Kaufmann moved to Southern California. A job as a gardener paid his bills until he found a position in 1916 as a draftsman for Reginald Johnson. Kaufmann soon proved his worth. In 1920 he was made an associate, and two years later Johnson formed a partnership with Kaufmann and Roland E. Coate. After designing many houses, St. Paul's Episcopal Cathedral in Los Angeles and All Saints Church in Pasadena, Kaufmann and Coate separated from Johnson to establish their own firms.

Kaufmann became a popular and prolific architect with over 400 commissions executed by his office within a ten-year span. His portfolio consisted of numerous magnificent mansions, college and high school campuses, resort hotels, theaters, and commercial centers. In addition to his work for Caltech, his best known projects were the Scripps College campus, the Los Angeles Times building, the Santa Anita Race track com-

Hall of the Associates.

plex and the architectural work for several dams, including the Hoover dam.

Bertram Goodhue, who Thomas A. Talmadge refers to as that "Ariel of architecture," felt that Spanish Colonial was an appropriate building style for a region settled by Spaniards. But Kaufmann, Johnson, Coate and Neff, using elements from different Mediterranean countries, created an eclectic architecture which became known as the "Californian style." Although there is no verification that Kaufmann traveled in Europe, he had a strong sense of the spirit of European architecture. According to Jan Furey Muntz, Kaufmann used "these [Mediterranean] details with consummate skill and an obvious understanding of the vocabulary rather than a superficial application of style."

Kaufmann's first task for the Caltech project was to establish the location of the Athenaeum. Two sites had been proposed: one was the corner of Hill Avenue and California Boulevard; the other would terminate the east-west axis of the campus. Fleming was adamant that it should be on the Hill-California corner. In an undated report presented to the administration, Kaufmann gave his reasons for choosing the central axis site. "The location on the central axis permits of an open scheme to the north and south, and, in effect, gives the building a better setting than the corner location." Moreover as the principal building of the residential section it would be appropriate for the Athenaeum to "close the most important axis on the campus."

Kaufmann struggled unsuccessfully to rework Goodhue's plan, which consisted of two main dining rooms, one to seat 240, the other 60, two small dining rooms, kitchen and service rooms, lounge, large library, writing room, men's and women's toilets and coat rooms, offices, bedrooms on the second floor and a billiard room and servant's quarters in the basement. Additional rooms such as a treasure room, lecture room, chess and card room, shower and locker room, porches and terraces were listed as "desirable." Kaufmann explained that if the scheme showing 40 single bedrooms and seven suites was reduced to 30 single bedrooms and four suites the cost could be reduced from $400,000 to $300,000. Moreover the number of bedrooms would dictate the layout of the first floor.

In his report Kaufmann expressed his frustration, "For the purposes of proceeding with this work, it seems to me that the location of the building should be definitely settled, a minimum requirement of accommodations be given me so that I may be able to proceed with a fresh start rather than to attempt to adjust the present plans." Once the requirements were established and Kaufmann was given a free hand to develop his own design, he created a building which fully justified Balch's magnanimous investment.

Caltech's Athenaeum is a rich blend of Italian villa and Spanish hacienda with overtones of rural Andalusia. Mounted on a plinth, the building has no definitive front, and each facade displays its own characteristics. The east elevation, which overlooks the residential area of Hill Avenue, is divided into three sections broken by an arcaded court. On the south side a "town" entrance consists of a grand porte-cochère modeled on Bullocks Wilshire's covered entrance, designed to accommodate the newly popular automobile. The portico is Italian Renaissance: classic columns with Corinthian capitals support chevron-edged arches; a double staircase leads to an entry door surmounted by a curved pediment framed by fancy finials.

"Gown" members enter the building from the west (campus) side through a loggia whose paired columns support ribbed groin vaults and form the open side of a Mediterranean-style inner courtyard, 60 feet square. Known as the West Patio, the space is the heart of the building surrounded by colonnades leading from dining rooms and entry hall. Andalusian influences are evident

Key to Seals in the Hall of the Associates. Twenty-five institutions are represented.

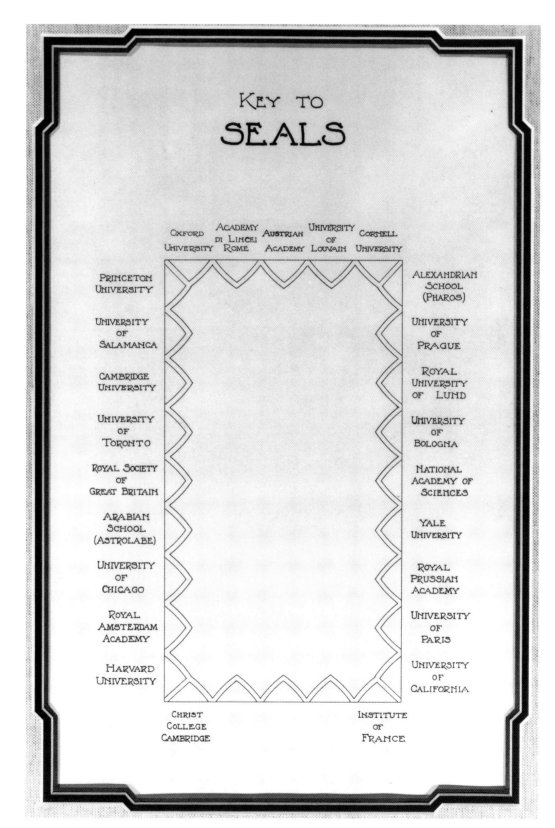

KEY TO SEALS

OXFORD UNIVERSITY

ACADEMY DI LINCEI ROME

AUSTRIAN ACADEMY

UNIVERSITY OF LOUVAIN

CORNELL UNIVERSITY

PRINCETON UNIVERSITY

UNIVERSITY OF SALAMANCA

CAMBRIDGE UNIVERSITY

UNIVERSITY OF TORONTO

ROYAL SOCIETY OF GREAT BRITAIN

ARABIAN SCHOOL (ASTROLABE)

UNIVERSITY OF CHICAGO

ROYAL AMSTERDAM ACADEMY

HARVARD UNIVERSITY

ALEXANDRIAN SCHOOL (PHAROS)

UNIVERSITY OF PRAGUE

ROYAL UNIVERSITY OF LUND

UNIVERSITY OF BOLOGNA

NATIONAL ACADEMY OF SCIENCES

YALE UNIVERSITY

ROYAL PRUSSIAN ACADEMY

UNIVERSITY OF PARIS

UNIVERSITY OF CALIFORNIA

CHRIST COLLEGE CAMBRIDGE

INSTITUTE OF FRANCE

The Athenaeum Lounge in the 1960s. For several years the lounge was home to a magnificent Persian rug, a gift from P. G. Winnett, president of Bullock's department store. Abbas Firouzi, the present owner of the Pasadena Rug Mart, identified it as a handknotted rug from the village of Birjand, county of Meshad, around 1880. An undated note in the Institute Archives explains that the rug was "woven for the palace of a Persian nobleman over a century ago, having taken twelve men twelve years to weave it...When the city of Masha in the province of Khorassan (the birthplace of Omar Khayyam), the home of the original owner of the rug, was threatened by Bolshevik uprisings, the rug was smuggled to a seaport under control of the British and thence to an Armenian merchant in New York." The historic treasure was eventually sold because its 47 by 28 foot size was too large for the Athenaeum lounge.

Right: Albert Einstein. The famous physicist and his wife, Elsa, stayed at the Athenaeum as guests of the Institute. Einstein was a visiting professor for the 1932 and 1933 winter terms.

in the red-tiled roof and white-washed walls, punctuated on the ground floor by tall windows covered with wrought-iron grilles. Balconies and a third floor loggia are reminiscent of Florentine villas.

The exterior's blend of classic elements flows into the interior rooms. Decorative features include a Greco-Roman entrance hall with a vaulted ceiling, an Italian Renaissance lounge, paneled in black walnut, and dining rooms with ceilings painted by Italian muralist Giovanni Battista Smeraldi.

The lounge's walnut paneling is repeated at two ends of the main dining room. This room's showpiece is a magnificent beamed ceiling painted in a style called grotesque, a fanciful decoration incorporating medallions, cherubs, and foliage. The style was popularized in the 16th century by Raphael and his followers, who were inspired by paintings on the walls of grottos found beneath the remains of Nero's grandiose palace in Rome.

The Hall of the Associates, named for the Institute's highly valued support group, was designed as a dining room and a lecture room. Lectures were held every Thursday evening on current topics ranging from new scientific discoveries to politics. Hale felt that it would add academic significance to the room if the seals of the world's principal institutions of learning were painted in arched panels around the perimeter of the Florentine-style coffered ceiling.

Hale, aided by professors Paul Epstein and William Munro, selected universities and academies which had made the most significant contributions to the progress of learning through research and discoveries. Institutes were eliminated if they failed to respond or send their coat of arms; if an Institute's seal could not be located; or if a seal was non-existent. Eventually twenty-five institutions were selected. In a letter to Munro (July 2, 1930) Hale writes, "You will notice that the head of Athena used by the Institute of France and the [London]

Athenaeum Club naturally do not differ much, except by facing in opposite directions, which is not an unfamiliar phenomenon in France and England."

An 18th-century Flemish Verdure tapestry, which hangs in the Hall of the Associates, was given to the Institute in 1951 by an anonymous donor. A Board of Experts from the Huntington Library wrote to Caltech's Trustees, "We believe that the tapestry would be a happy decoration for a dining room which often is used for after-dinner speaking. The beasts in the garden being presumed edible or, if not edible, at least symbolic of a commodity which in the coming months and years, may become increasingly scarce on the table, may have a charming and nostalgic effect on future diners..."

A curving travertine stairway takes visitors to the second floor guest rooms. Kaufmann's proposed 30 rooms had become 23 single bedrooms, now all doubles. A third floor loggia, open to the elements on the campus side, originally served as a sleeping porch for graduate students who paid $10 a month for the privilege of shivering through winter's morning mists. At a meeting of the Athenaeum Board of Governors on February 18, 1975 it was decided to eliminate the use of the loggia because "it was not appropriate ..to furnish such low-quality housing."

The building's four suites were assigned to distinguished visitors or more permanent residents. The southwest suite was named the Einstein suite after the famous physicist and his wife, Elsa, stayed there when Einstein was a visiting professor for the 1932 and 1933 winter terms. But the suite was originally designed as an apartment for Arthur Fleming, who paid for the paneling in the living room. He chose white mahogany over walnut because it was cheaper.

In her review of Kaufmann's work for a Scripps College exhibit, Muntz wrote about the Athenaeum's interior, "As the architecture itself is so rich, the decoration of the

Detail of the porte cochère. This classic style Corinthian capital features acanthus leaves and sunflowers.

interior requires only the simplest addition of furniture and a few well-placed oriental rugs." At a meeting of the Executive Council on May 31, 1930, "Mr. Balch expressed his desire that the furnishing be done under the advice of one person so that it will be a unified scheme of decoration ... and that after the furnishing is completed, there be nothing put into the Athenaeum in the way of busts, additional furnishings, etc. without consultation with him." George W. Reynolds was the chosen interior designer.

The staircase hallway, or Hall of the Presidents, serves as a portico to the main lounge and dining room. Its walls are decorated with portraits of the Institute's leaders. Although the Balchs' name was never attached to a Caltech building, their generous gift is recognized with a copper plaque in the lobby, portraits in the lounge and busts in specially designed niches on the West Patio.

The Athenaeum's inaugural functions were not without problems. At the first dinner for members and their wives held on October 30, 1930, Millikan and Robert Daugherty, a professor of engineering, spent most of the evening in the basement trying to get the furnace to work. But nothing could cloud the glory of Caltech's new social center. The formal opening was delayed until February 4, 1931, so that Albert Einstein could attend. Other important guests that day included leaders of the associated institutions and two more Nobel Laureates, Albert Michelson and Robert Millikan.

With its massing, spatial arrangements, emphasis on light and shade, and blend of Mediterranean features, the building is a fitting closure for the east end of the main campus axis. According to Muntz "the Athenaeum acts like a giant jeweled buckle catching the contours of the earth and containing the edge of the campus." Hale's vision, the Balchs' generosity and Kaufmann's successful design gave Caltech the richest gem in its architectural crown.

The Library of the
Athenaeum doubles as a
private dining room.

CHAPTER FOURTEEN

Undergraduate Dormitories

"Now it was the promise of the Board of Trustees that should it ever be necessary to move the building and fireplace, the face bricks would be carefully taken down and would form the face of another fireplace at another site."

— *Grant V. Jenkins to Donald S. Clark, October 25, 1958.*

For many years Caltech's undergraduates were scattered in different locations. Some rented rooms in the surrounding neighborhood, others lived on campus in a simple frame building which became known as "The Old Dorm." This two-story, 20-room chalet-style building was designed by Myron Hunt and Elmer Grey in 1910 as a $26,000 Boarding Hall "under close oversight of proper instructors" for the boys of Throop Academy. Originally located at 289 North Los Robles Avenue, the dormitory was moved to the new campus in 1915. To facilitate the move, architects Sylvanus Marston and Garrett Van Pelt had the building cut into seven sections. It was then placed on a new foundation at the east end on the north side of the main axis to avoid interfering with the permanent dormitory. Goodhue's plan ignored the "moved Dormitory." He considered the site awkward and the wooden building temporary.

In 1924, trustee Robert Roe Blacker and his wife gave $5,000 to build a student union hall to be connected by a ramp to the dining room. Henry Greene, of the architectural firm Greene and Greene, designed the hall as a handsome wooden bungalow containing a single 40 x 50 foot room with a hardwood floor. The students quickly named their new building The Dugout, after a campus shed of the same name where two students had run a sandwich shop. Grant V. Jenkins '24, Student President, led a committee to raise money for furnishings. Modeled after the wall of carved initials at Britain's Eton College, the fireplace of The Dugout featured bricks engraved with students' names (guaranteed by a one dollar donation). The finished fireplace included 398 personally inscribed bricks, 22 donated by clubs and miscellaneous donors, with other furnishings (mantel, hearth, andirons) provided by faculty members and student classes. On January 23, 1924 the building was dedicated and the first fire lit.

As part of the plan for the new student dormitories built in 1931, existing fraternities were disbanded leaving a need for a non-resident student club. In 1934, Mrs. Millikan raised the funds and, in consultation with Myron Hunt, organized the remodeling of

"The Old Dorm" with orange trees, 1917. Originally located on North Los Robles Avenue, this dormitory was designed in 1910 by Myron Hunt and Elmer Grey for the boys of Throop Academy. In 1915 it was moved to the new campus.

The Throop Club fireplace. To help raise money for furnishing the Throop Club, students paid one dollar to have their names inscribed on bricks.

Henry Greene's bungalow. The Dugout became the Throop Club, a place for off-campus students to eat lunch and hold gatherings. The Club remained an important part of Caltech life until the Winnett Student Center was constructed on the site of the Old Dorm in 1962. The "named bricks" were incorporated into its south wall and all Southern California brickholders were invited to the dedication.

THE SOUTH STUDENT HOUSES

"THESE HOUSES ARE TO ACT AS CENTERS FOR THE STUDENT LIFE OF THE INSTITUTE, FOR WE HOPE TO MAKE NOT ONLY THE HOME LIFE, BUT THE INTERNAL ATHLETICS, AND ALL THE FRIENDLY RIVALRIES AND COMPETITIONS OF THE STUDENTS, CENTER AROUND THEM."

— *Robert Millikan to Harry Chandler, February 6, 1929.*

In 1928 a committee was appointed by the Board of Trustees to study the problem of undergraduate life at the Institute. It consisted of Robert Millikan, Arthur Noyes, William Munro, and eleven faculty and students representatives. Four seniors, three juniors and two sophomores made up the student section of the committee. Robert Lehman, President of the Student Body, together with students Phillip Schoeller and Walter Scholtz, were given three months leave of absence to study residential conditions at universities in Europe and the United States.

With all expenses paid, the group visited Oxford, Cambridge and London Universities in England; Cité Universitaire in France; University of Toronto in Canada; and in the United States: Annapolis, Chicago, Cornell, Duke, Harvard, Haverford, MIT, Pennsylvania, Princeton, Swarthmore, West Point, Williams and Yale. Aided by their committee members they composed a detailed document on student life. It was published in the 1931 Caltech Bulletin.

The Institute's policy of limiting undergraduate enrollment, small group instruction, and its emphasis on cultural values influenced the committee's recommendations. In a five-page document addressed to the Board of Trustees on March 21, 1928 the committee included the following points: mass housing and mass dining should be avoided; national fraternities should be discouraged; a series of residence halls with no more than 75 students in each was recommended; units should be semi-divided by separate entries so small groups of student rooms (approximately 25) would have the opportunity of developing comradeship in a close-knit setting; the Institute should have control over assignments to the groups but take into consideration the desires of individuals.

"In this way all the real merits of the fraternity housing system can be obtained, without incurring the serious evils which that system brings with it. The several housing units would inevitably develop a certain amount of loyalty and would develop among themselves a wholesome rivalry in outdoor sports." In a letter (July 21, 1928) asking Mr. F. C. Austin, a new member of the Associates, if he would like to become a donor for one of the houses, Millikan wrote, "In these halls we hope to get the students to live in intimate and democratic but highly stimulating and cultural relationships."

In addition to the grouping of student rooms, the committee recommended, "the proper provision for supplying with wholesome food, under agreeable conditions." Although it would be more expensive, they stressed the importance of avoiding typical large college commons and recommended that food be served in small dining rooms which might share a common kitchen. The committee estimated the cost of each 75-student unit at $200,000.

Eight units with 75 students in each would accommodate Caltech's 600 undergraduates. Millikan was proud of the fact that the Institute had done its homework. Caltech was going to learn from the mistakes of other American universities by trying to establish ideal housing. Millikan's aim was to be as successful as the colleges at Oxford and Cambridge universities. However, he believed it would be wise to

test the new concept before trying to find money for all the units. He decided to begin with construction of four units along California and bordering the south edge of the main campus axis.

On February 6, 1929 Millikan wrote to Harry Chandler, owner of the Los Angeles Times, asking his help in finding donors. Joseph Dabney had already agreed to put up a Dabney Hall but Millikan needed "three other public spirited men of Southern California" to match Dabney's offer. Millikan emphasized his eagerness to complete the campus according to the plan "growing out of Mr. Goodhue's genius." The astrophysics group had been funded and would be built shortly, which together with the student dormitories and the Athenaeum would complete the southern and eastern edges of the campus. "The Institute.. will ultimately be the central and dominating feature architecturally of this region."

Eventually Millikan obtained the necessary funds from Mr. and Mrs. R. R. Blacker

South Student Dormitories, Kaufmann's original perspective view with a tower. The tower was never built. The dormitory complex is made up of low horizontal buidings which define the spaces within.

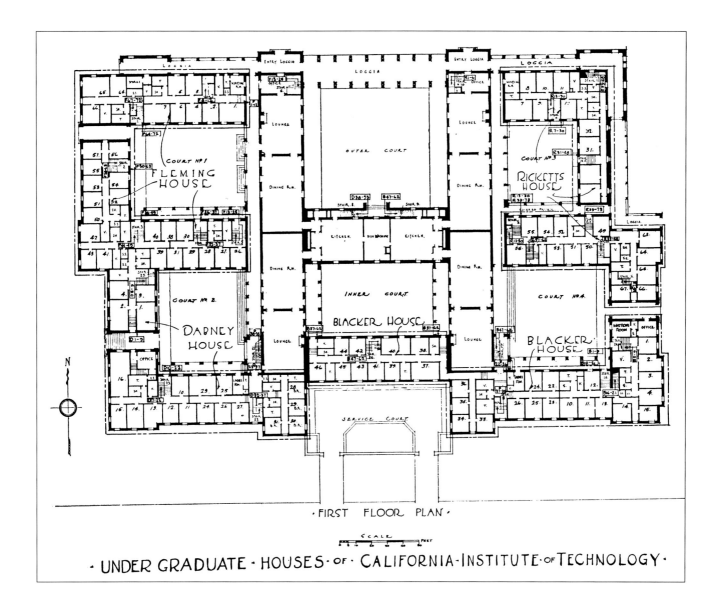

· FIRST FLOOR PLAN ·

SCALE

· UNDER·GRADUATE · HOUSES · of · CALIFORNIA·INSTITUTE·of·TECHNOLOGY ·

who had given money for a student union, and Dr. and Mrs. Louis D. Ricketts. Both men were trustees. Funds for the fourth house were provided by twenty additional donors, including Joseph Dabney. The house was named for Arthur Fleming who, as President of the Board of Trustees from 1917 to 1933 had become deeply involved in the life of Caltech. For many years he had maintained that the students should be housed in one area.

Bertram Goodhue's letter to Hale (June 5, 1923), in which he mentioned that he was sending blueprints for the dormitory

section, explained that he had succumbed to Fleming's stipulation. His plan would house all the undergraduate students in one location. "As you will see, it's entirely based on a system of patios, some big and some little, the central one being very considerable in size, surrounded by the highest dormitories...In the center of the main court, the octagonal affair is a bandstand, with above, space for tubular chimes, the latter being a pet idea of Mr. Fleming."

Gordon Kaufmann, who was selected in place of the Goodhue Associates as the architect for the dormitory complex, developed

First floor plan of Student Dormitories. Kaufmann organized the four houses around six courtyards. Small groups of rooms with separate entrances linked to the overall framework of a house wrap around the private space of an inner courtyard. Communal rooms border an outer and inner central courtyard, with a single kitchen forming a bridge between the housing groups.

Detail of arcade capitals
decorated with scientists,
aviators, musicians and
sportsmen.

An arcaded loggia links
Kaufmann's dormitory
complex to the main east-
west axis of the campus.

Goodhue's "system of patios" into a brilliant arrangement of Mediterranean-inspired buildings and courtyards that fully satisfied the committee's requirements.

The design of the dormitory group uses the same architectural style as the Athenaeum. Whereas Caltech's social center was created as the dominant mass isolated by the space around it, the student center is made up of low horizontal buildings defining the spaces within. Like courtyard houses in Muslim architecture the outside form of the complex camouflages the inner plan. Kaufmann organized the four houses around six courtyards. Within each courtyard separate entrances led to small groups of rooms. Lounges and dining halls flank an outer and inner central courtyard. A single kitchen, accessible to all four dining rooms, forms a bridge between the housing groups. An Andalusian-style facade featuring a white-washed wall with a scalloped edge, windows with wrought-iron grilles, and a pair of tiled staircases disguises the service section.

The dormitory's south elevation, broken by delicately arched loggias on the second floor, blends into the residential environment of California Boulevard. Access is restricted to a central service court because the boulevard is a public street. The main entrance to all four houses is through two monastic-like passages which open into an arcaded loggia flanking the main east-west axis of the campus. This covered way repeats the portales of Goodhue's academic buildings. However, in contrast to Goodhue's simple square pillars, Kaufmann used columns with decorative capitals composed of scientists, musicians and sportsmen.

John H. Hood, who graduated from Caltech in 1921, cast all the capitals for the dormitories out of structural concrete using a mixture of crushed dolomite and cements. The product was then cut with air tools to simulate natural stone. An article in the November/December 1979 issue of Caltech's *Engineering and Science* discussed the origin of the capital characters. According to Hood, "Kaufmann did not try to caricature anyone in particular. 'If they resemble someone, it is purely coincidental as my men did not have a picture to help them in their finishing.'"

To create a separate identity for each house Kaufmann used an eclectic mix of decorative details, and imbued all the architectural elements, arcades, loggias, arches, columns, capitals, tympanums, pediments, and plaques with personality and humor. Joseph Giovannini wrote, "Each court was an enclosed world and a visual discovery."

On the south side of Blacker House courtyard the Ionic capitals of rectangular piers that support a loggia are decorated with figures, some gripping flasks, others holding garlands. Entry doors to the lounge and dining room are framed by Moorish-style portals whose columns are topped by jovial figures.

The courtyard of Ricketts House contains an unusual abundance of terra-cotta. The inside of five arches bordering the entry passageway are lined with terra-cotta; two doorways leading to student rooms are framed by elaborate Moorish-style arches of terra-cotta. Inside the rope borders of one arch figures of men, owls and monkeys sit in the branches of a grape vine. The capitals of the other arch show two men involved in different activities of academic life.

Ricketts House arcades. The arches bordering the passageway are lined with terra-cotta squares decorated with leaves and rosettes.

STET FORTVNA DOMVS

In keeping with an inscription "Labore et Honore" chosen by Fleming, the architectural elements of Fleming House are dignified and restrained. A doorway opening onto the campus is surmounted by a broken pediment and the name of the house. Loggias on two side of the courtyard are composed of columns with Corinthian capitals and pedestals with leaf-like feet at the corners.

An egg-shaped plaque over an archway on the west side contains a pelican, an emblem used in heraldry to represent Christ.

A rectangular entryway with a rosette frame leads from a pathway bordered by orange trees on the west side of Dabney House. On one side of the inner courtyard are Romanesque arches with erudite figures on pedestals terminating each pilaster.

Opposite: Ricketts House courtyard. The terra-cotta arch surrounding a dormitory door has capitals composed of two men looking at each other over a stack of books; one man is playing a saxophone and the other is blocking his ears.

Dabney House's rectangular entryway is bordered by rosettes. The Dabney name is set in a temple-like niche below a Moorish-style second floor loggia, where squatting figures holding books guard the corners of a balustrade.

Romanesque arches inside the Dabney House courtyard. Between the arches are medallions illustrating different modes of transportation.

Above the rounded pediment of the citrus entry is a ceramic bas relief which looks like a scientific version of "The Last Supper."

On March 24, 1933, Kaufmann was awarded Certificates of Honor by the Southern California Chapter of the American Institute of Architects for his designs of the Athenaeum and the Undergraduate Dormitories.

A bas relief in Dabney House courtyard which looks likes a scientific version of "The Last Supper." Pasteur, Newton, Copernicus, Archimedes, Euclid, da Vinci, Franklin and Darwin, each holding a symbol of his achievement, give obeisance to a god-like central figure whose head is framed by the rays of the sun. Perhaps intended as a representation of Galileo, the scientific god has been renamed Feynman, in honor of Caltech's Nobel Prize-winning physicist and revered teacher.

Landscaping
the Early Campus

"THE WHOLE CAMPUS SHOULD BE SO OBVIOUSLY A UNIT, WITH ITS OAKS AND CAREFULLY CHOSEN GROUPS THAT THE TREATMENT SHOULD BE CAREFULLY THOUGHT OUT AND PLANNED FOR DENSITY AND MASS EFFECT, AND THE VARIOUS COURTS SHOULD BE WORKED OUT AS PARTS OF THE DESIGN, FINER IN DETAIL AND MORE INTRICATE IN CHARACTER."

— Beatrix Farrand to Arthur Fleming, March, 1928

To take full advantage of the site, with its contours and native trees, the early leaders of Caltech stipulated that the architecture should be an integral part of the landscape. Part of the original 22 acres (from Wilson Avenue to Holliston Avenue), which Arthur Fleming purchased and gave to Throop Polytechnic in 1908, had been a golf links for the Hotel Green. The plot was extended to Hill Avenue with the purchase of an additional eight acres in 1922.

In a letter to Goodhue (October 5, 1915) President Scherer stressed that the existing live oaks should "govern the layout of the buildings." Approximately 40 oak trees covered the site. According to Fleming about 28 would remain after all the buildings were constructed. Today there are about sixteen. Although Fleming envisioned date palms lining the grand approach from Wilson to the planned Memorial Building, Goodhue felt that the stately elegance of Italian cypresses was more appropriate for his Taj Mahal-inspired scheme. Installed in 1928, these trees were the sole element of any landscaping plan. At first they made a delicate, wispy statement, but as they grew and thickened they were groomed into sturdy sentinels with carefully rounded tops.

A 1912-1913 student publication reports that the "12 acres of orange groves" produced a bumper crop which the students disposed of during an orange fight. The groves covered most of the land east of Throop Hall. An early photograph shows the Old Dormitory with an orange tree orchard in the foreground.

As the construction of the academic portion of the campus was being completed, Beatrix Farrand became involved in some of the landscape design. Born in 1872 in New York, Beatrix Caldwalader Jones was the only child of wealthy parents who separated when their daughter was twelve years old. Beatrix was educated by private tutors in the artsy setting of her mother's New York apartment. At the end of the 19th century there were few opportunities for women to pursue formal courses in landscape architecture. Instead Beatrix learned from an apprenticeship with Charles Sprague

Four hundred-year-old
Engelmann Oak. President
Scherer stressed that the
existing live oaks should
"govern the layout of the
buildings."

Sargent, director of the Arnold Arboretum in Boston. In their 1985 book, *Beatrix Farrand's American Landscapes*, Balmori, McGuire and McPeck use Beatrix's own words to describe how she learned from Sargent "to make the plan fit the ground and not to twist the ground to fit a plan." Beatrix expanded her education by studying paintings of classical landscapes and visiting gardens in Europe. A small clientele made up of her mother's friends rapidly formed the foundation of a successful business. By 1896 she was considered one of America's outstanding landscape architects. Her many commissions encompassed private residences, university campuses, and botanical gardens. Her clients included Mrs. Theodore Roosevelt, Mrs. Woodrow Wilson and John D. Rockefeller. One of her best known, finest and still intact projects is Dumbarton Oaks in Washington, D.C.

In 1913 Beatrix Jones married Max Farrand, a professor of history at Yale, who became the director of the Huntington Library in 1927. Although the Farrands moved to San Marino, Mrs. Farrand retained her east coast offices, traveling continuously while doing much of her work on the train. Farrand was aware that her gender put her at a disadvantage in a male-dominated business world, so she made sure that every aspect of her work was executed in a professional manner. But in spite of her professionalism and extensive experience in designing college campuses, she struggled for recognition at Caltech. Except for payment for laborer's time and planting materials, she was never paid for her services. However, the Institute was desperately short of funds because most of Fleming's endowment was lost in the collapse of the stock market.

Farrand's main work was the design of the garden for the Dabney Hall of the Humanities. She was concerned that there was no overall landscaping plan. In a letter to Fleming (March, 1928) she wrote, "As I think over the question of the court of the Humanities Building, it seems to me that

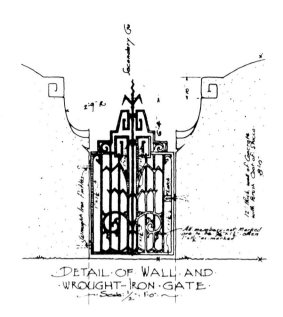

DETAIL·OF·WALL·AND·
·WROUGHT-IRON·GATE·
Scale: ½: 1'·0'

Architect's drawing of Dabney Garden's Mayan-inspired, wrought-iron gate. It guarded an opening in the west wall but is no longer there.

Right: Dabney Garden, designed by Beatrix Farrand. She created an enclosed garden with a lawn, olive trees, climbing roses, benches and a tiled fountain. In the early 1980s the garden was renovated by Land Images. Farrand's original stepped design and olive trees remain, but a central walk which divided the lawn was changed to a perimeter pathway.

the problem is a very interesting one with delightful possibilities of beauty and seclusion. It should, however, be a part of the campus, perhaps slightly different in character but related to it in the general scheme of planting." Her solution was to create an enclosed garden within an open campus, using skillfully pruned olive trees whose delicate silver leaves contrasted with the gnarled wood of the tree trunks. A tiled fountain, teakwood benches, Cherokee roses climbing up stone walls, a Mayan-inspired wrought-iron gate, a carpet of grass, and the soft green canopy of trees made this secluded space a "seductive Spanish garden."

For ten years Farrand remained involved on a part-time volunteer basis with the landscaping of the campus. She wrote to

Millikan (November 15, 1932), "I hope the Institute will allow me to keep a watch on the garden [Dabney] in which I am so interested. (I need hardly say there will be no charge for the time I spend in doing this work.)" In 1935, William B. Munro, chairman of the Building and Grounds Committee, asked Farrand to develop a plan for the landscaping of the western end of the campus provided there would be no charge. For the central plaza she suggested planting some rapidly-growing trees surrounded by a hedge, with groups of small trees on either side, to give a temporary identity to the space of the proposed central library. She also proposed planting a large tree in each corner of the plaza, and filling the central space with beds of ice plant divided by temporary walkways. In 1936, she suggested that a gateway on the east side of the Gates Annex garden be moved to align with the Dabney gateway "so that a vista through the two gardens can be obtained."

In addition to making sketches and suggesting plantings for several areas around the academic buildings, Farrand became involved in the planning of the area south of Arms. The architects designed the Arms area on two levels, Farrand recommended one level. When Farrand's ideas for Caltech's landscape clashed with the Goodhue Associates, the administration decided the architects should make the final decision regarding walls, walks and grading. Farrand selected the plantings. Eventually the Executive Council had to rescind their vote when Mrs. Robinson, the wife of Trustee Henry Robinson, donor of one of the buildings bordering the area, said she preferred the one-level plan. In a letter to Farrand (November 19, 1938) Munro wrote, "The levels, etc. have been arranged...in accordance with your recommendations, although the architects strongly urged a different plan." He asked her to specify the plantings and to choose an appropriate spot for a live oak tree to be donated by the class of 1937.

After ten years of consultation, and having her ideas rejected and her specifications changed, Farrand tired of her unpaid advisor status. On March 24, 1938, she suggested to Millikan that given her increased role she should receive a small annual fee of $100, plus $50 for expenses. Millikan replied by offering to make her a Caltech Associate. She refused, "I do not feel it possible to accept as there would be an ever present consciousness of not having a real right to be one of the group." She was more forthright about her unhappiness to Munro, "As you have doubtless realized...my present half-charitable, half-amateur status is not satisfactory." After her husband died in 1940, Mrs. Farrand returned to the east and terminated her association with Caltech.

The Athenaeum project had the advantage of an ample budget with additional expenditures allocated for landscaping, parking and tennis courts. To create an aesthetically appropriate setting, Kaufmann suggested that the Institute hire landscape designers Florence Yoch and Lucile Council. He was confident in their ability having worked with them on several of his residential projects, including his own house.

Florence Yoch was born in 1890 and grew up in Santa Ana, California. Unlike Beatrix Farrand she enrolled in an academic program in landscape architecture at the University of Illinois, Urbana-Champaign. Her education was supplemented by courses at Cornell, the University of California and her travels. She began practicing in 1918. Her first partner was Lucia Fox, succeeded by Lucile Council with whom she developed a highly successful business. Yoch and Council worked with the best architects of the period. Myron Hunt described them as "able, highly-trained, much-traveled and experienced women."

James J. Yoch describes the scope of his cousin's work, "She designed gardens for historical adobes from San Gabriel to Monterey, grand villas and manors in Los Angeles and Santa Barbara, traditional and contemporary homes in Pasadena, parks at Shoshone Falls and in Orange County, a botanical garden in Mexico, and the sets for five movies, including Tara in *Gone with the Wind.*"

Florence Yoch was blessed with creative vision, Lucile Council with business acumen. Both women had high standards and expected the same of their employees. They hired women as well as men, but a female employee would be fired if she married. Yoch and Council pioneered the transportation of large trees, enabling many of their gardens to have a mature appearance from the beginning. Yoch's designs found their inspirations in the gardens of Europe. According to Robert Smaus, Yoch's work "became an important link in a chain of garden design that leads from the villas of Italy and the Moorish gardens of Spain to the Mediterranean landscape of Southern California."

Yoch created a perfect setting for the Athenaeum, Caltech's new social center and architectural masterpiece. Her design combined grandeur with an ambiance that represented the building's Mediterranean architecture and the natural landscape of California.

Two different scenes were assembled for the main approaches to the building. The automobile entrance was placed to the side on Hill Avenue, leaving space at the California Boulevard corner for graduate housing which was never built. In place of a somber avenue of cypresses, typical of the approach to a European estate, Yoch used closely-spaced and dramatically-tall lemon-scented eucalyptus trees creating an airy border for the main driveway. For the campus approach to the Athenaeum, which also serves as the north edge of the student dormitories, Yoch designed an avenue of olive trees shading a brick path. Council carefully

matched each tree, selecting trunks that were especially twisted and knotted to add to the sense of antiquity and to give the impression of walking toward a villa in the Tuscan countryside. A band of sturdy sycamores disguises the service entrance and shields the tennis courts from the north side of the building. Tall cypress trees provide a canopy for a pathway to San Pasqual Street. In contrast to these major plantings, the building itself is framed by date palms and a variety of bushes, shrubs and vines. Firethorn, lemonade berry, tobira, hawthorn, ivy, clematis, trumpet vines, and beds of Spanish jasmine provide color, texture and perfume.

Yoch's use of large areas of recreational green space between the dormitories and the Athenaeum helps emphasize the isolation of the social center. In recognition of the building's architectural richness, she used restraint in her selection of trees and plants for the enclosed courtyards of Kaufmann's buildings. "An olive, a cypress, lady palms, and a garland of vines" create a sense of intimacy for the Athenaeum's central gathering place. Planters, simple lawns and a few carefully selected trees suffice for the secluded courtyards of the student dormitories.

Despite the lack of a grand scheme as suggested by Beatrix Farrand, Caltech's early campus benefited from the skill of two women considered to be among America's leading landscape architects. Sensitively designed informal courtyards provided quiet retreats for study and contemplation in contrast to the entrances marked by the stately cypresses of the West Court academic area and the graceful eucalyptus of the Athenaeum's social center. Until the balance of the landscaping could be installed, beds of delicate perennials replaced the proposed reflecting pools, and squares of cumbersome ice plant filled the central court.

Opposite: Athenaeum
Carriage entrance.
Florence Yoch used closely-
spaced and dramatically-
tall eucalyptus trees to
border the driveway.

Athenaeum's Olive Walk.
Yoch designed an avenue of
olive trees for the campus
approach to the
Athenaeum. She was
inspired by the landscaping
of Tuscany.

In the spring of 1939 a California Native Garden was established on two acres of undeveloped land at the northeast corner of the campus near Wilson Avenue and San Pasqual Street. The area was designated for future additions to Biology and Chemistry. In the interim, a garden of California plants would serve to screen a parking lot and provide specimens for research in plant physiology. Theodore Payne, who had 40 years experience in the collection, propagation and hybridization of native species, was hired to assist in the selection and design. Known as the Old Garden, the area remained intact until the construction of the Norman W. Church Laboratory in 1955.

By 1940, all that remained to complete Goodhue's master plan and fulfill Hale's dream of a unified campus was the domed Memorial Building and its reflecting pools. The Athenaeum and student dormitories completed the east end, the astrophysics group finished the south edge, and buildings for biology, geology and chemistry completed the west and north borders. Unfortunately the flow of funding and the impetus for construction, which had already been interrupted by the economic depression of the 1930s, was again affected by the outbreak of a second world war.

Athenaeum's west lawn. Large areas of recreational green space between the dormitories and the Athenaeum help emphasize the isolation of the social center. Yoch's lone cypress tree selected for the West Patio grew too tall and has been removed.

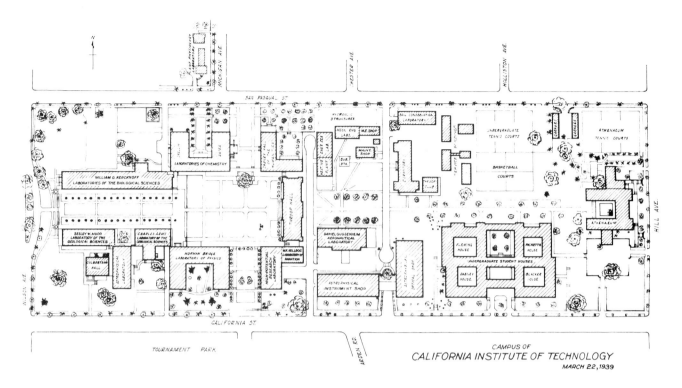

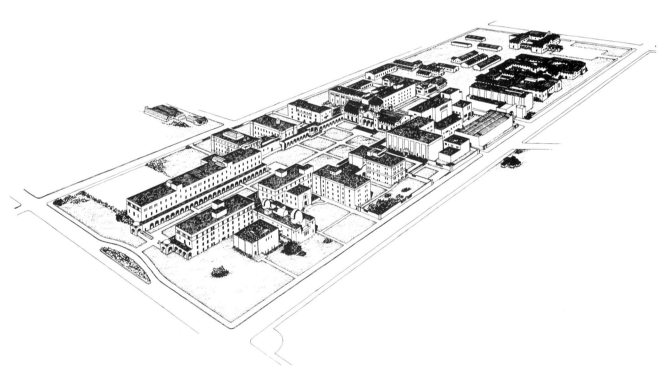

Campus Map, 1939 and three-dimensional Campus Map, 1945. Except for the central Memorial Building and its courtyard with reflecting pool, the Goodhue Master Plan (combined with Kaufmann's residential section) was almost complete. The Old Dorm, Throop Club and a few temporary war surplus huts used by physical plant would be replaced by additional student dormitories.

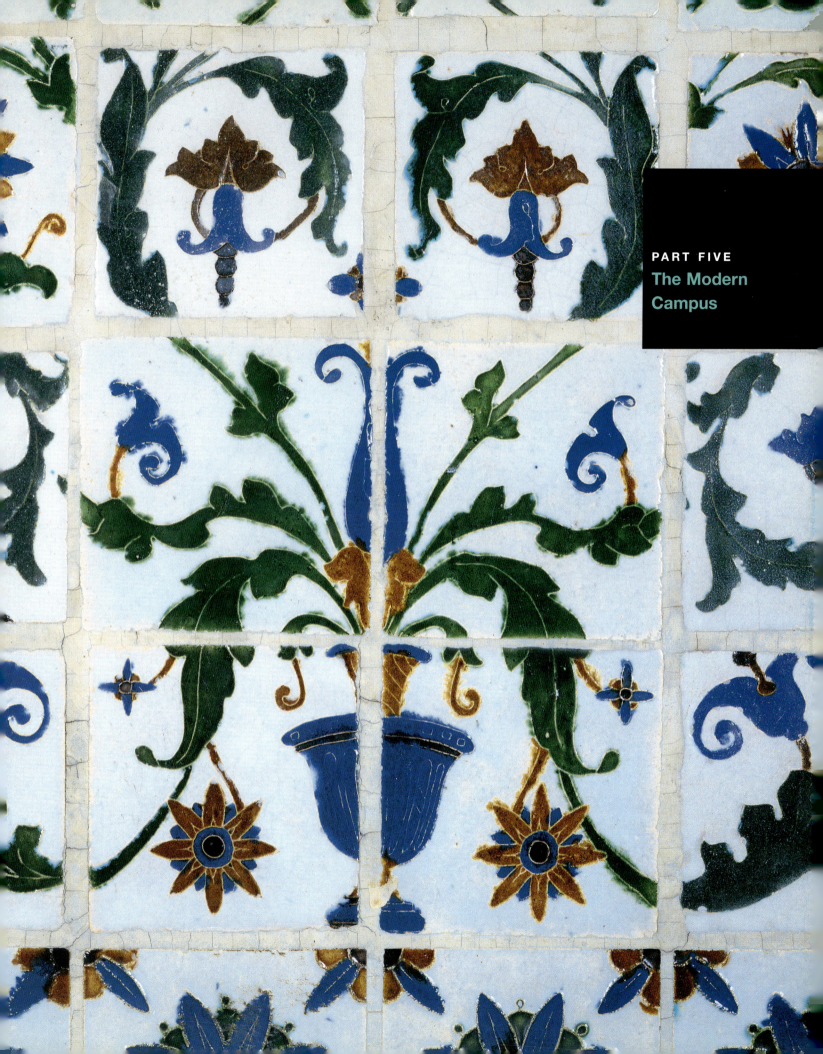

Changing of the Guard

From the late 1930s to the mid-1940s Caltech lost several leaders and major donors, and went through many changes. Death took chemist Arthur Amos Noyes in 1936, and biologist Thomas Hunt Morgan in 1945; trustees Henry Robinson in 1937, George Ellery Hale in 1938, Arthur Fleming in 1940, and Allan Balch and his wife Janet in 1943. In 1940 Goodhue's architectural firm, Mayers, Murray and Phillip, dissolved. During the war Millikan's health deteriorated and his ability to run the school suffered. His retirement in 1945, at the age of 78, signaled the end of an era.

Hale's ambition to establish a first-rate college of science and engineering had been fully realized under the guidance of Millikan. But how would this small, select school cope with the post-war challenges? Progress in the sciences, especially physics, had suffered as the Institute spent its time and energy on war-related research. Under Millikan the building and research program had depended on funding from individuals and foundations. Where would the support come from now? Would government support, which had been acceptable during the war, take away academic freedom and independence?

The Institute's postwar future was put into the hands of Lee Alvin DuBridge, who became Caltech's first President (Millikan had been Chairman of the Executive Council) on September 1, 1946. DuBridge was born in 1901 in Terre Haute, Indiana. Following undergraduate studies in physics at Cornell College in Iowa, DuBridge took only four years to get through masters and doctorate programs at the University of Wisconsin. After two years as a National Research Council fellow, supervised by Millikan at Caltech, he held teaching positions at several universities. In 1940, he accepted a position at MIT as head of the National Defense Research Committee's radiation laboratory. Under his management the laboratory made important contributions to the role of radar during the war.

DuBridge's scientific work was excellent, but it was his organizational skills which made him the perfect choice to move Caltech away from its military involvement and back into the academic world of teaching and research. In his 1946 annual report

Lee Alvin DuBridge became Caltech's first President (Millikan had been chairman of the Executive Council) in 1946, and remained at the helm for 22 years. DuBridge brought the Institute out of its military involvement of World War II and back into the academic world of teaching and research.

DuBridge summed up the war years, "The Institute ...gave itself over completely to helping win the war." Now, with money that had been put aside while the government was paying for research dedicated to the military, DuBridge raised faculty salaries and established a twelve-month salary plan. In the following years he introduced key people to help rebuild the divisions. Robert Bacher, who was hired to strengthen the physics division, became Caltech's first Provost in 1962. Jesse Greenstein created an astronomy department, separate from the observatory staff. Robert Sharp established the new field of geochemistry within the Division of Geology. George Beadle, chairman of biology, together with Linus Pauling, chairman of chemistry, established the new field of chemical biology. Hallett Smith increased the offerings in humanities to include the social sciences.

DuBridge believed it was possible to maintain the independence and integrity of scientific research even when supported by government grants. Judith Goodstein explained in *Millikan's School* that in order to further his cause DuBridge became expert at "explaining science to the public, presidents and members of Congress."

The Pereira Luckman Plan

"As funds become available for the construction of new athletic facilities, new dormitories, or new laboratories, the location and general design will have been planned in advance with a view to a coherent development of the entire campus."

— *Lee DuBridge quoted in Engineering & Science, December 1952.*

Except for the construction of a government-funded Hydrodynamic Laboratory connected to Guggenheim in 1941, Caltech's building program came to a standstill during the war years. In 1945, a Mechanical Engineering building, flanking the east-west axis across from the Guggenheim laboratory, was designed by the physical plant department. Later the building was named for Franklin Thomas, a former Dean of Students and a distinguished civil engineer.

In 1952, architects Pereira and Luckman were hired to prepare a master plan. In 1959 their firm split and Charles Luckman Associates continued advising Caltech until 1964. Pereira and Luckman organized the placement of buildings, defined a style of architecture and prepared sketches, but different firms were hired to execute the designs. Compared to the definitive statement of Goodhue's master plan and the richness of Kaufmann's residential section, the modern campus became an eclectic mix of functional buildings.

During the 1950s Pereira and Luckman specialized in corporate projects, such as CBS Television City, Robinson's Pasadena and the Signal Oil Company Office Tower. After the office divided, William Pereira worked on buildings for Occidental College, and a master plan for Pepperdine University. His best-known design is the Los Angeles County Museum of Art.

Although Charles Luckman trained as an architect, he began work as a salesman and by the age of 37 was president of Lever Bros. After returning to his original profession he became well known as an architect, civic leader and supporter of education. Projects executed by his firm included the Cape Canaveral Space Center in Florida, the Johnson Space Center in Houston, and the new Madison Square Garden in New York. Successful designs in California included the Los Angeles Convention Center and the futuristic theme restaurant for Los Angeles' new airport in 1962.

In addition to a change in Caltech's leadership the war had introduced a radically new approach to architecture. At the turn of the century architects began to reject the ornate revivalist architecture and machine-made frills of the 19th century. A Modern

Movement evolved out of the British Arts and Crafts and Continental Art Nouveau. During the inter-war period German architects Walter Gropius, Ludwig Mies van der Rohe, and Dutch architect J. J. P. Oud, used the new industrial materials of structural steel and reinforced concrete to create cubes and towers of stark simplicity.

Le Corbusier's expressionist architecture in France and Frank Lloyd Wright's organic dwellings in America offered alternative visions to Modernism. But in the mid-1940s and 1950s the Modern Movement, also known as the International Style, began to dominate American architecture. Just before World War II Walter Gropius and Ludwig Mies van der Rohe fled Germany to become practitioners and teachers in America. According to John Morris Dixon, in a 1988 editorial in *Progressive Architecture*, the buildings of the International Style "appeared to herald a bright future, liberated from the weight of tradition." A universal modernism now replaced architecture with regional distinctions and historical references.

In developing a new Master Plan for Caltech, Pereira and Luckman proved that they were Modernists, but like other architects of the 1950s and 1960s they rebelled against the starkness of the International Style. According to Dixon, some critics felt that "the triumphant new architecture would blanket our world with flat-surfaced, flat-topped, neutral-colored modular containers that no amount of fine Miesian detail could redeem from monotony."

For several years George Beadle, chairman of biology, and Linus Pauling, chairman of chemistry, had wanted a building where they could establish a joint chemistry-biology research program. Following an article about the proposed program in the *Los Angeles Times*, Norman W. Church telephoned DuBridge to express his interest,

"Dr. Millikan has been trying to get money out of me for 20 years, but I never knew what I wanted. Now I do know and it is a building for your chemistry-biology work."

For three decades Church was known as California's biggest breeder of Roughbred racehorses. Legend states that he felt indebted to the Institute because a Caltech chemist helped to exonerate him from accusations that he had drugged one of his horses. According to DuBridge's oral history the chemist was Linus Pauling, but Arnold Beckman remembers that it was he who was responsible for getting Church out of his predicament.

Church wanted his building, which was located on the southeast corner of Wilson Avenue and San Pasqual Street, to be large, to bear his name, and to be designed by Stiles O. Clements, one of California's premier architects and a keen horseman. Clements created a bare-bones, functional building with decoration limited to a diamond patterned steel grille over the two entrance doors.

These buildings were only a small part of the academic growth which DuBridge realized was needed in order to reestablish Caltech's role in the fast-changing world of scientific research. DuBridge felt that filling in gaps in the original Goodhue plan was not sufficient. The Institute must embark on an ambitious expansion and grow beyond its original boundaries.

With a goal of $16.1 million, Caltech launched its first major fund raising campaign in 1958. A professional firm was hired to run the campaign and the theme "Unconquered Worlds" was adopted. Donations ranged from $1,000,000 given by an anonymous donor to a contribution of $10 from a schoolboy. George Stiny wrote to Robert Bacher, chairman of physics, "I am now 12 years old, and in the seventh grade at Thomas Starr King Junior High School. My ambition is to attend Caltech and study physics...I read in the *Los Angeles Times* about Caltech's Development program. I would like to take part in that program. Enclosed is the small sum of ten dollars."

The campaign brochure stressed the importance of Caltech's role in scientific research. "Our country is now engaged in a world-wide technological contest for military security, for economic stability and growth...We must avail ourselves of the most profound scientific knowledge — the kind of knowledge that extends to the innermost mechanics of the atom and to the farthest reaches of interstellar space. Likewise, we must develop engineering concepts and techniques of the highest order."

At such a time it is not surprising that DuBridge raised the question of whether some of the Goodhue buildings should be rehabilitated or torn down. "High Volts could be patched up temporarily for the physicists or torn down to make room for a new five-story laboratory adequate for both physics and mathematics." He went on to suggest that Gates Laboratory of Chemistry and Throop Hall, which were outdated and not especially earthquake resistant, might be demolished.

Norman W. Church Laboratory for Chemical Biology, 1956, north entry door. Architect Stiles O. Clements created a plain, functional building with decoration limited to a diamond-patterned steel grille over the entry doors.

NORMAN W CHURCH
LABORATORY FOR CHEMICAL BIOLOGY

CHAPTER SEVENTEEN

Plain and Decorated Boxes

"THE TOTAL BUILDING PROGRAM WILL REQUIRE SOME FIVE YEARS TO COMPLETE. BY THAT TIME WE WILL HAVE THE FACILITIES REQUIRED TO ENABLE CALTECH TO CONTINUE ITS PROGRAM OF BEING ONE OF THE FINEST — POSSIBLY THE FINEST — BUT NOT THE LARGEST SCHOOL OF SCIENCE AND ENGINEERING IN THE WORLD."
— *Lee DuBridge at the groundbreaking ceremony for Physical Plant, September 16, 1958.*

In Pereira and Luckman's master plan an auditorium connected to Goodhue's annex Culbertson Hall was sited at the corner of Wilson Avenue and California Boulevard. A central library, to accommodate the fast-growing needs of the Institute, would take the place of Goodhue's undefined Memorial Building. Wings for aeronautical engineering would be added to Guggenheim. Other new buildings planned on the original campus plot included a mathematics and physics building, an annex to link Kerckhoff Biology to the new Church Laboratory of Chemical Biology, additional undergraduate dormitories, and a student center with coffee shop. On the newly acquired land north of San Pasqual Street there would be a graduate housing complex, physical plant department buildings and a new engineering building.

Pereira and Luckman executed renderings of the buildings proposed in the 1958 campaign. Their designs set the tone for Caltech's modern campus. Laboratory buildings were plain boxes lacking the warmth and refinement of Goodhue's Moorish inspired creations. Walls of smooth or textured concrete punctuated by steel-framed windows and unadorned entrances replaced Spanish stucco and historical decoration.

The campus expansion north of San Pasqual Street began with a ceremony on September 16, 1958, to break ground for the physical plant department which had previously been housed in war surplus huts. DuBridge stated, "A significant element of this new program is the acquisition and use of a large area on the north side of San Pasqual Street." According to the news release of the ceremony, "the actual groundbreaking was accomplished by a signal from Explorer IV, (one of a series of U.S. scientific satellites) picked up as it made its pass over Pasadena early this morning. The signal was transmitted to a relay switch which, in turn, started the engine of a giant power shovel."

In the early 1960s functional buildings for new laboratories followed in quick succession. Alles Laboratory of Molecular Biology (1960) linked Kerckhoff and Church laboratories. The glass-roofed Campbell laboratory (1960) was added to the Earhart Plant

Bertram Goodhue's 1923 High Voltage Research Laboratory was converted into Sloan Mathematics and Physics in 1960. The facade was stripped clean of its delicate diaper pattern as floors and windows were added. Only light fixtures remind us that a noble sculpture of two men creating a bolt of electricity once framed the entrance.

Rendering by James Perry Wilson of the Goodhue Associates' 1930 proposed extension to the West Kerckhoff building. Unadorned boxes of the 1950s and 1960s would now take the place of Goodhue's Moorish-inspired architecture.

Alfred P. Sloan Laboratory of Mathematics and Physics, 1960. Architects Holmes and Narver were responsible for the reconstruction. The Navy had given the physicists a ten-million-volt Van de Graaff accelerator which had to be housed in the basement, so the mathematicians, who had been scattered in different buildings, were given the upper three floors.

Research facility ensuring that Caltech would remain a world center of innovation in plant biology. Pereira and Luckman designed the Karman Laboratory of Fluid Mechanics and Jet Propulsion (1960), a two-story addition to Guggenheim which sits on top of the 1941 Hydrodynamics Laboratory. With money from the Alfred P. Sloan Foundation, the High Voltage building was converted to Mathematics and Physics (1960). The shell of the building was preserved, but the principal features of Goodhue's design were destroyed.

Although most of the new campus buildings were simple boxes, some architects experimented with decorative surfaces to create diversity. Charles Luckman and Associates enlivened the facade of the Keck Engineering Laboratory (1961) with panels of porcelainized enamel over aluminum. The original plans called for the use of several colors but in the end only red was used. The building was funded by the W. M. Keck Foundation and the Superior Oil Company.

Pereira and Associates decorated the north facade of the Firestone Flight Sciences building with a repetitive motive of concrete blocks. The inspirations for this design element came from window grilles in Moorish architecture, or the Mayan designs copied by Frank Lloyd Wright.

Neptune, Thomas and Associates took decorative surfaces a step further when they designed the Booth Computing Center with a textured wall featuring circular bumps. The students immediately named the building "Mammary Hall." At a meeting of the Board of Trustees on October 7, 1963, it was stated that "the round surfaces on the south face of the building are felt by some members of the Buildings and Grounds Committee to be not in keeping with any other architectural features on the campus." The architects agreed to cut down the circular bumps with chipping hammers. In 1969, the same architects used overlapping rectilinear shapes simulating shingles to decorate the Downs and Lauritsen Laboratories of

Architect's rendering of
Keck Engineering, 1961.
Panels of porcelainized
enamel over aluminum
were to be in several colors, but only red was used.

Physics, which replaced the Machine Shop
and Porter's arch facing California Boulevard.

Chester Carlson, an alumnus and inventor of the Xerox process, made a substantial
gift to the Institute which became the major
source of funds for the Noyes Laboratory of
Chemical Physics. At the dedication on May
6, 1968, Earnest Watson called the building
"a temple of science," honoring Arthur
Amos Noyes who had so strongly influenced
the development of Caltech. Designed by
Risley, Gould and Van Heuklyn, the building
is a stark box except for the east facade
which has tall, vertical windows terminating
in hooded arches.

One of the Institute's most pressing
obligations was to provide more housing for
students. By the mid-1950s more than half of
the 675 undergraduates and nine-tenths of
the 490 graduates lived off campus.
Kaufmann's dormitories, which had been
intended for 75 students, now accommodat-
ed over 90 students in each house. As previously planned, an additional complex
designed by Smith, Powell and Morgridge
would be built on the north side of the
Olive Walk. Since the new complex would
be close to Kaufmann's Mediterranean eclectic complex, the Buildings and Grounds
committee felt that it was important to
spend the money for comparable buildings
with red-tiled roofs. But the north houses'
pebble-faced balustrade supported by precast columns and pierced concrete block
screens bears no resemblance to Kaufmann's
intimate arcade with its figurative capitals.

Adjacent to the new undergraduate
housing would be a Student Center for
which Mr. P. G. Winnett had already pledged
$400,000, a dining hall funded by the Harry
Chandler family, and a coffee shop. Because
the graduate residences would be located
away from the original campus, costs could
be kept to a minimum. As a result the four
graduate houses, which form an "L" on the
north-east corner of Holliston Avenue and
San Pasqual Street, have flat roofs and
unadorned facades.

Left: Firestone Flight Sciences Laboratory, 1962. Students think the pattern of the concrete blocks represents tire tracks because the building was funded by the Firestone Tire and Rubber Company.

Below: George W. Downs Laboratory of Physics and Charles C. Lauritsen Laboratory of High Energy Physics, 1969. The Downs wing was built with funds provided by Mr. George W. Downs and the National Science Foundation. The Lauritsen wing was built with Atomic Energy Commission funds and named for Dr. Charles C. Lauritsen, a member of the Institute faculty from 1930 to 1968.

Plain and Decorated Boxes

Rendering of Arthur Amos Noyes Laboratory of Chemical Physics, 1967. Tall, vertical windows terminating in hooded arches relieve the starkness of this box-like building. It was dedicated to Arthur Amos Noyes whose vision and painstaking work so strongly influenced the development of Caltech.

Rendering of Undergraduate Dormitories. Although these 1960s buildings were designed to reflect the Mediterranean architecture of Kaufmann's student housing, the pebble-faced balustrade and concrete block screens are typical of the post-war era.

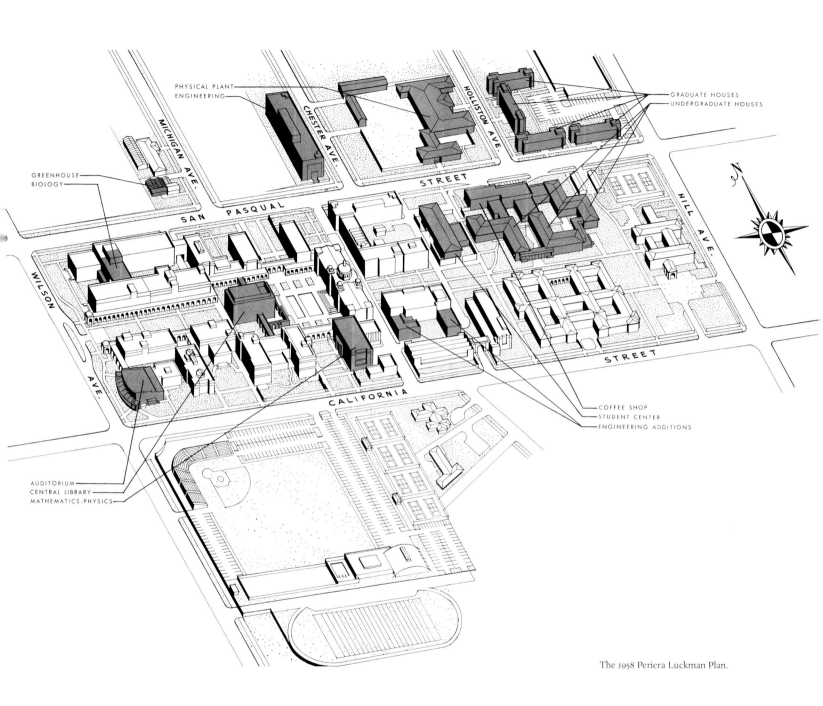

PHYSICAL PLANT
ENGINEERING

GRADUATE HOUSES
UNDERGRADUATE HOUSES

GREENHOUSE
BIOLOGY

MICHIGAN AVE.

CHESTER AVE.

HOLLISTON AVE.

HILL AVE.

SAN PASQUAL

STREET

WILSON AVE.

STREET

COFFEE SHOP
STUDENT CENTER
ENGINEERING ADDITIONS

CALIFORNIA

AUDITORIUM
CENTRAL LIBRARY
MATHEMATICS-PHYSICS

The 1958 Periera Luckman Plan.

CHAPTER EIGHTEEN

An Auditorium

"It is surely a thing of great and delicate beauty, inside and out...Mr. Stone...was enormously pleased, and says it is the best thing he has done...The moral of all this is that, if you want an artistic creation, you may have to put up with a few engineering and budgetary headaches."

— *Lee DuBridge to Dr. James R. Killian at MIT, March 2, 1964*

Since 1921 audiences had been crammed into tiny Culbertson Hall for concerts, plays, debates and lectures. For any large gathering which could not be held outdoors, Caltech had been forced to use the Pasadena Civic Auditorium or public school auditoriums.

Pereira and Luckman's rendering for a 1,200 seat auditorium was markedly different to the designs of Bertram Goodhue and the Goodhue Associates. In place of a Spanish-style building which would have been attached to Culbertson Hall, Pereira and Luckman drew a contemporary two-story auditorium with cables holding a roof cantilevered over an entry patio. In addition to the main hall there would be small lecture and conference rooms, practice rooms and an interdenominational chapel. Arnold and Mabel Beckman responded promptly to the 1958 Campaign by offering to pay for the auditorium, whose cost at that time was estimated at $850,000.

Arnold Beckman had been associated with Caltech since 1923 when he enrolled as a graduate student. He received a Ph.D. in photochemistry in 1928, served on the facul-ty until 1940, then left to establish his own business, Beckman Instruments, Inc. Beckman is regarded as one of the world's top inventors of instruments which are used in scientific and medical fields. In recognition of his work the National Academy of Sciences awarded him their highest honor, the 1999 Public Welfare Medal.

In 1953 Beckman was the first alumnus to be elected to Caltech's Board of Trustees. Before becoming Chairman of the 1958 Development Fund Program, Beckman had been Chairman of the Buildings and Grounds Committee. From 1964 to 1974 he was Chairman of the Board and now serves as a Life Trustee and Chairman Emeritus.

All those involved agreed that because the auditorium would become Caltech's link with the public it should be a "Monumental Structure." Therefore location and design became of paramount importance. Early in 1960 Dr. Beckman approved the selection of the internationally famous architect, Edward Durell Stone.

Stone's projects spanned the globe, from the Museum of Modern Art in New York and the Kennedy Center in Washington

1930 Rendering by James Perry Wilson for the Goodhue Associates updated design of Bertram Goodhue's original auditorium to be connected to a small reception wing (built and named Culbertson Hall). After it was decided to extend the geology buildings all the way to Wilson Avenue, the auditorium was shifted further south. This design, with its decorative beamed ceiling, would have been in keeping with the Spanish theme of Culbertson Hall.

D.C., to the United States Embassy in New Delhi and the United States Pavilion for the World's Fair in Brussels. Stone believed that architecture should be timeless. He liked order and always searched for the simplest and most direct solution to a plan.

After careful consideration of several prime locations, it was decided to place the auditorium at the intersection of the newly extended north-south axis and a future east-west axis at Constance Street. It would become a prominent landmark at the north end of the campus with the Athenaeum defining the east side and the Scott Brown Gymnasium marking the south end. Moreover the building would be easily accessible to the public, and there would be adequate parking. The original site at the northeast corner of California Boulevard and Wilson Avenue could be reserved for academic buildings.

However, as plans for the building developed, a problem arose with its location. There would be insufficient space around

1958 Rendering by Pereira and Luckman for a modern auditorium on the corner of Wilson Avenue and California Boulevard. The estimated cost was $850,000.

Aerial view of Edward Durell Stone's Beckman Auditorium before any neighboring buildings were constructed. In a book on his own work Stone describes the building as "an all-white circular structure resting on a podium placed at the end of a broad mall lined with olive trees and flower beds. A peristyle of 32 tapered, diamond-shaped columns with capitals flared to support the roof overhang, completely encircles the reinforced concrete building. The diamond pattern on the exterior wall is repeated on a smaller scale inside...The ceiling of the main hall is a mesh of small disks, suspended tent-like from the apex of the conical roof; gold in color, it dominates the white and gold scheme which, except for the red carpeting, prevails throughout the building."

the building unless Michigan Avenue could be moved approximately 25 feet to the west. To do this Caltech would have to get permission from the City, acquire unneeded properties, and pay the cost of realigning the street. When the City Planning Commission rejected the proposed change, Caltech's Buildings and Grounds Committee decided to move the auditorium 30 feet to the east, placing it slightly off the main north-south axis.

In a memorandum to DuBridge (June 17, 1959) a Faculty Planning Panel recommended that the building be rectangular in shape and compatible in style with existing buildings. They felt it should be orientated south with promenade porches on three sides including an especially wide terrace on the south which could be used as a stage for outdoor gatherings. The uses of the building were listed in order of importance: "distinguished speakers, demonstration lectures, convocations, smaller conferences in connection with convocations, musical activities, dramatic activities." A list of functional requirements included a note about acoustics, "Acoustics planning should be

such that no amplification be required, but amplification should be available for special purposes."

Stone was a romantic architect, and a strong proponent of New Formalism. This style reflected certain classical elements and used restrained decoration in opposition to the Miesian "less is more" philosophy. For Caltech's Beckman Auditorium in dramatic opposition to the Planning Panel recommendations he created a temple-like structure set against the backdrop of the San Gabriel mountains. Stone may have been influenced by a trip he had just made to North Africa, including Ethiopia, where he would have seen round churches with conical roofs.

Before the building was completed but after the design had been fully developed it became apparent that the acoustics were not ideal. In a letter to DuBridge (November 22, 1961), Vern O. Knudsen, an acoustical engineer at UCLA, who had been called in to advise on the problem, stated, "It does seem to me strange indeed for one of the foremost scientific and technological institutions in the world to place appearance above function." Both the circular shape and volume of

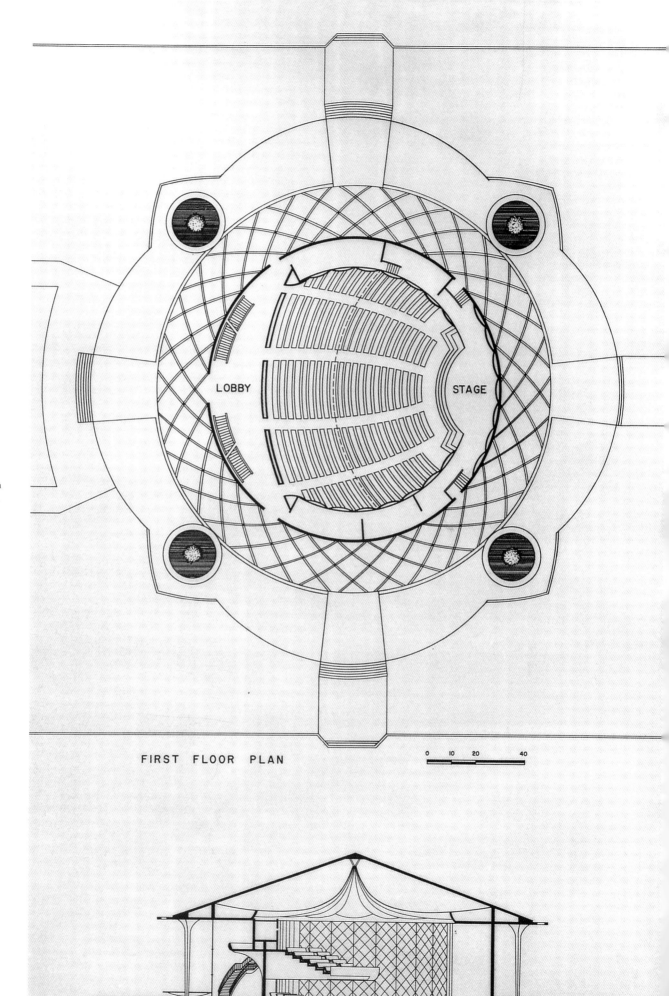

Plan and Section
of the Beckman
Auditorium

LOBBY STAGE

FIRST FLOOR PLAN

0 10 20 40

The white conical roof of Beckman Auditorium repeats the effect of the snow covered mountains in the background. A sprinkler system on the roof facilitates maintenance.

The opening ceremony on February 25, 1964, was carefully orchestrated to show off the beauty and features of the new structure. After a talk entitled "From Spanish Tile to Modern Stone: Some Recollections" by George Beadle (who had left Caltech in 1961 to become President of the University of Chicago), remarks by President DuBridge and the donor Arnold Beckman, and a performance by the Glee Club, everyone agreed that the acoustics were surprisingly good.

For many the auditorium was a disappointment because it was designed primarily as a public lecture hall, not as a performance venue. It lacked adequate theatrical lighting, wing space, back stage dressing rooms and toilet, storage, staging area or lift to transport heavy items from the delivery door to the stage. "The consensus was that the magnificent aesthetic success of the Auditorium had hampered its utility." In the following years some adjustments were made and the auditorium has become the center for a wide variety of productions. According to the 1998 brochure of the Performing Arts Series, "Musicians, dancers, and actors from around the globe come to the Beckman Auditorium bringing the richness of world cultures and up-to-the minute satire, zany humor, and spellbinding tragedy. On this campus, play is an essential element."

the building were counterproductive to good resonance. Dr. Floyd R. Watson, who was the acoustical consultant for the project, worked hard to overcome the building's drawbacks. Sound absorbing material on walls, floor and ceiling combined with a high quality amplification system saved the auditorium from serious defects.

The Beckmans gave unstintingly to meet the final cost which was just under $1.5 million, considerably higher than the original estimate. The auditorium, which DuBridge proudly described as "a thing of great and delicate beauty," won a Pasadena Beautiful award and strengthened the liaison between the campus and the community.

CHAPTER NINETEEN

A Central Library

"IT IS A PLEASURE FOR ME TO HAVE THE OPPORTUNITY TO HONOR A GREAT MAN AND A GREAT SCIENTIST. I LOOK FORWARD TO THE PLANNING AND CONSTRUCTION OF THIS BUILDING WITH GREAT INTEREST, WITH THE FERVENT HOPE THAT IT WILL BE MOST AGREEABLE TO ALL WHO MAY USE IT."
— *Dr. Seeley Mudd to Mr. Ruddock and Dr. DuBridge, March 24, 1959.*

From April 1948 to May 1949 the office of Gordon Kaufmann and J. E. Stanton worked on preliminary plans for a library building on the site of Goodhue's Memorial Building. When Kaufmann resumed practice as an architect after serving in the war he became an adherent of the International Style. Kaufmann's plan consisted of two basements, five floors and a penthouse. The upper floors rested on a broad base which filled the west flank of the central quadrangle. Although lacking Goodhue's elaborate dome and Churrigueresque decoration, Kaufmann's cubistic design might have been a reasonable solution, but the drawings were never used.

Gordon Kaufmann's, 1949 preliminary design for the central library. The upper floors formed a modernistic cube resting on a broad base which filled the west flank of the central quadrangle. Arcades below the north and south wings followed the form of Goodhue's portales. Funds were unavailable and the plan was never used.

Pereira and Luckman's rendering of the central library published in the 1958 Campaign brochure. The design is a modification of Kaufmann's cube-like structure. A courtyard with a reflecting pool would fill the space between the library and Throop Hall. "DuBridge does not wish to see the library building restrict the campus area within the central plaza, any more than necessary."

Below: Charles Luckman's 1959 rendering of the central library. "The exterior of the building, though setting a new style on the campus, will be in harmony with neighboring structures. The cast-stone screen that envelops much of the surface brings to a central focus comparable motifs in other buildings."

Funds were unavailable, and in 1949 Kaufmann died at the age of 61.

In February of 1953 the Institute's Ways and Means Committee discussed the need to raise $1.5 to $2 million for a central library. The existing main library in Bridge Annex had long since overflowed its capacity. Books were stored in corridors, attics, basements and underground steam tunnels. Pereira and Luckman were asked to draw plans, and according to a meeting memorandum of April 12, 1954, "All present from Caltech agreed that the exterior should blend with the surrounding buildings." After seeing the first set of sketches DuBridge felt that eight floors were too high in relation to the surrounding buildings. Pereira and Luckman adjusted their drawings to show a 50,000 square foot building of six stories and a penthouse to house 420,000 books. At a meeting of the Board of Trustees on July 12, 1954, DuBridge stated that the "library should be a memorial to the late Robert A. Millikan."

Pereira and Luckman were asked to give the project their personal attention because the building would be an important architectural feature of the campus. During the next few years they produced additional drawings, but the Institute's effort to raise the money was unsuccessful. The 1958 Campaign brochure included a rendering, which was a modification of Kaufmann's cube-like structure surrounded with a wall punctuated by arcades on each side. After William Pereira and Charles Luckman separated in 1959, Charles Luckman Associates drew a final version of the library eliminating the arcades, but incorporating a sun control grille to cover the east and west facades. The design was similar to the cast stone panels on Firestone Laboratory. However, the Board of Trustees Minutes (February 2, 1959) stated that "the library contract can be canceled at the Institute's option upon completion of preliminary plans because it was necessary to delay final selection of the architect until funds were in hand."

Finally, at a meeting of the Board on April 6, 1959, DuBridge said, "The big news of the week [is] the gift by Dr. Seeley G. Mudd of funds to provide the Robert A. Millikan library." Dr. Mudd pledged an amount not to exceed $2.4 million. In a letter addressed to Mr. Ruddock, President of the Board, and Dr. DuBridge (March 24, 1959) he laid out his conditions.

"It is understood that I am the sole donor of the building. It is agreed that I will be entitled to approve the architect, the plans, the specifications and bid form, the contractor and final bid with alternates, including all change orders. In addition I shall be entitled to approve the furniture and equipment up to a maximum of $400,000.

The dollar value of this gift shall remain as confidential as possible and hereafter will not be released to the press or otherwise publicized.

Mr. Ruddock said it would be appropriate to place a donor's plaque at the entrance of the building. This too I should like to approve.

Out of respect for Dr. Millikan and his educational standards the California Institute of Technology will make every effort to maintain the library in a dignified manner; for example, students and others using the library will be prohibited from smoking in the library except in one or two rather small designated rooms on each floor, or from placing their feet on library tables or chairs, and from consuming food or beverage anywhere in the library except for Board members during Board meetings and for library personnel who may use a small area for coffee breaks."

Seeley G. Mudd was the brother of Harvey S. Mudd and the son of Colonel Seeley Wintersmith Mudd. In 1931, after completing his training as a physician, Seeley Mudd became a Research Associate in Medical Chemistry at Caltech. Using the super voltage x-ray machine (it operated up to 750 kilovolts) in High Volts and later in Kellogg Laboratory, he participated in the pioneering studies and treatment of deep-seated malignant tumors in patients from the County Hospital. From 1935-1945, Dr. Mudd was Professor of Radiation Therapy with an office in North Mudd, the building which was dedicated to his father. After an interlude as Dean of the USC Medical School he returned to Caltech in 1959 as a Research Associate in Medical Chemistry.

Millikan Library towered over Throop Hall. As predicted by Alan Blumenthal, the building dwarfs its neighbors.

He had joined the Associates in 1928, and was a member of the Board of Trustees from 1960 until his death in 1968.

Dr. Mudd expressed general approval of the interior arrangements of the building as proposed by Charles Luckman. But three years later, at a meeting of the Board of Trustees on August 28, 1962, it was announced that the Institute, with the approval of the donor, had signed an agreement with Flewelling and Moody, an established Los Angeles architectural firm experienced in designing school, college and civic buildings.

Dr. Mudd wanted the library to represent a significant memorial to his dear friend. In searching for a model he may have looked at Ralph C. Flewelling's 1928 design of the Colonel Seeley Wintersmith Mudd Memorial Hall of Philosophy at the University of Southern California. According to David Gebhard and Robert Winter in *Los Angeles, An Architectural Guide* "the high campanile of this complex was [originally] the dominant vertical element of the campus."

To strengthen the Spanish theme of his Master Plan Goodhue had created a closed central courtyard similar to universities in Spain. His domed Memorial Building would have formed the west side opposite Throop Hall on the east side. But with only a grove of trees to mark the site of the future central building, the campus community had become used to the openness of the west court mall leading up to Throop Hall. Initially, DuBridge had rejected Pereira and Luckman's plans for an eight story building, but he now agreed that a tall tower would take up less green space and would solve the problem of the visual barrier created by a lower and longer building.

When plans for a library tower in the center of the campus became public several faculty members and students expressed their concern. Alan Blumenthal wrote to DuBridge, "The library building would not only ruin the most attractive vista on campus but a building of that height would certainly be out of scale, architecturally, resulting in a visual 'dwarfing' of the surrounding buildings." (February 10, 1965)

Concerned that similar protests might be expressed when the Institute asked the City of Pasadena for a zoning variance to permit a nine-story structure, DuBridge wrote a letter of explanation (March 19, 1965) to the faculty. For the people who felt that the new tower should be located elsewhere he wrote, "During all of these last forty-five years each revision of the campus master plan has reserved this space for the central library — to be located at the 'hub' of the campus. We are in the position of having built those buildings which constitute the 'wheel' without as yet having acquired the 'hub'." In defense of the design he said, "Mr. Ralph C. Flewelling...made a very careful examination of the entire campus, and built a model of it in order to test various design possibilities. He recognized the need for keeping the mall as open-looking as possible, at the same time designing a structure of fine external appearance and adequate for our library needs for a decade or more in the future. The donor himself generously devoted a very large amount of time to studying the design problem in collaboration with the architect and with campus representatives. The aim of all was to arrive at a structure both functional, useful, architecturally handsome, and a suitable monument to Dr. Millikan."

Most of the Institute's separate departmental libraries were consolidated into the new 63,000 square foot central building. Each discipline is housed on a separate floor with reference books and general reading material on the ground level. Rare books, originally shelved in a butternut-paneled room on the first floor, are now housed in the Institute Archives in the sub-basement of the Beckman Institute.

The Robert A. Millikan Memorial Library designed by architects Flewelling and Moody and completed in 1967. The donor, Dr. Seeley Mudd, selected the architects and became deeply involved in the design. According to Arnold Beckman, "He spent untold hours and hours worrying himself about details." The east and west elevations are faced with black granite from South Africa. The north and south facades are made up of grey-glass windows alternating with cellular-shaped precast white cement panels made from molds created by sculptor Malcolm Leland. The stones in the reflecting pool came from Baja California and were chosen for uniformity of size.

Dr. Mudd requested a spacious board room. The room's full height cast aluminum doors, designed by sculptor Malcolm Leland, open into the octagonal space. Carrara marble was used for the dedication plaque in the board room's lobby. To complete the setting, a pond and fountain on the east side of the building screen the noise of the city and recall Goodhue's plan for a reflecting pool in the west court. At a meeting of the Board of Trustees on August 1, 1966, a proposal by H. V. Neher to install a Foucault Pendulum on the west curved panel was rejected.

The original plans for the Institute's central building were interrupted by an economic depression, a war and a ten-year search for a donor. The final solution, a nine-story concrete, glass and granite-clad monolith, is strikingly dissimilar to the surrounding Spanish stucco academic buildings. If a tall monument had been required in Goodhue's time we might have had a version of the elegant tower topped by a dome which he designed for the Nebraska State Capitol. Instead, a building which represents architecture's post-war modernism would be Dr. Mudd's tribute to Millikan.

Interior of the Millikan Board Room with Throop Hall visible through the windows.

CHAPTER TWENTY

The Alexander Plan

"THESE SKELETAL CONCEPTS WILL ESTABLISH THE FORM OF THE CAMPUS AND PROVIDE A BASIC FRAMEWORK FOR PLANNING WITHOUT COMMITTING THE INSTITUTE TO THE DETAILS OF FUTURE PLANS OR TO PRECISE LIMITS OF THE CAMPUS."

— *Robert E. Alexander. Master Plan Report 1971*

At the end of December 1968, after 22 years at the helm of Caltech, Lee DuBridge resigned to become President Nixon's Special Assistant for Science and Technology. He was succeeded by Harold Brown.

Brown was born in 1927 in Brooklyn, New York. After receiving his undergraduate and graduate degrees in physics from Columbia University he moved to the west coast to join the research and development team at the University of California's Livermore Radiation Laboratory. A directorship at Livermore led to a position in Washington, D.C. as Director of Defense Research and Engineering for the U.S. government. In 1965, Brown became Secretary of the Air Force under President Johnson.

Charles Luckman had terminated his architectural consulting contract with Caltech on January 1, 1964. According to the Board of Trustees minutes he stated that the "campus master plan...is now in good order and quite adequate for the foreseeable future." Two years later Robert E. Alexander was hired "to work on long-range plans of

the campus, help in decisions on architects for new buildings, and coordinate all architecture and campus planning."

Robert Evans Alexander was born in New Jersey and did his architectural training at Cornell University. He established his own practice after World War II and later formed a partnership with Richard J. Neutra. According to his obituary in the *Los Angeles Times* (December 2, 1992) Alexander "was one of the most respected architects and planners in the nation, whose innovative ideas for affordable housing produced the Baldwin Hills Village in Southwest Los Angeles."

In addition to the responsibilities outlined by the Buildings and Grounds committee, Alexander stipulated that he should be the executive architect for one or two major buildings.

The Campus Planning Committee had recommended using San Pasqual street as a dividing line for two distinct areas of the campus: undergraduate activities would be concentrated south of the street and specialized research facilities to the north.

Harold Brown, President of Caltech from 1969 to 1977. Before coming to Caltech he was Secretary of the Air Force under President Johnson. He left to become Secretary of Defense under President Carter.

Architect Robert Alexander's rendering of the Court of Man. Humanities and Social Sciences building is on the east flank and Behavioral Biology on the west. The 1968 campaign brochure stated that "the California Institute of Technology believes that man's future is hopeful to the extent that he progresses in the understanding of his own behavior."

Following these requirements, Luckman's plan showed a functional design with open malls and throughways. Although he was involved in only the first phase of development north of San Pasqual, he suggested expanding the campus to Del Mar.

Following the success of the 1958 campaign which had exceeded its goal, a new development program, called Science for Mankind, was launched in 1967. The goal was $85.4 million to pay for new construction, rehabilitation of existing buildings, endowments for professorial positions and support for scholarly research and study. The makeup of the student body stood at 835 undergraduates and 700 graduates.

To create a suitable approach to the new Beckman Auditorium, the Alexander Plan created a large open space to be called the Court of Man, with a humanities and social sciences building on the east flank and behavioral biology on the west. An additional engineering building would form the north side of an engineering court established by Keck Laboratory on the west and Steele Laboratory on the east. To enhance the new campus setting created by the Alexander Plan, Caltech obtained permission from the City to close San Pasqual Street and parts of Michigan Avenue and Chester Street.

Adding to the geology grouping of North Mudd and Arms, the plan's southern section included a geophysical sciences building on the corner of Wilson Avenue and California Boulevard. Sloan Mathematics and Physics would acquire a small annex building for applied mathematics. A general

Throop Hall was damaged in the 1971 Sylmar earthquake. Interior and exterior walls revealed serious cracks.

services building, and a second gymnasium to augment the athletic facilities would be located south of California Boulevard.

In the 1980s, a cluster of graduate houses, originally planned for a site on Holliston Avenue, was replanned on Catalina Avenue between San Pasqual Street and Del Mar Boulevard. Previous plans designated one of the Holliston houses as a residence for newly admitted undergraduate women. However, before the first 25 women arrived in the fall of 1970, it was decided "to bring the women as closely as possible into the mainstream of campus life." An area adjoining Dabney and Blacker houses was renovated and separated, but each woman would belong to one or other of the houses.

As construction of this new phase was getting under way the residents of Los Angeles were awakened on the morning of February 9, 1971, by a devastating earthquake. A few days later President Brown announced "the recent earthquake was the most severe in the history of the present campus. Throop Hall evidenced considerable cracking of partitions and exterior filler walls, both of hollow tile construction. No basic structural damage has occurred, however."

DuBridge had expressed concern about the earthquake resistance of Throop Hall and Gates Laboratory of Chemistry as early as 1957. On December 30, 1968, engineering faculty members George Housner and Paul Jennings sent a memorandum to Royal Tyson, campus architect, summarizing a seismic report on Throop Hall by a Mr. Dysland. "If the ground shaking is significantly stronger than in 1952 [Tehachapi earthquake] the tile filler-walls forming the exterior walls of the building and the interior tile partition walls can be expected to shatter and possibly collapse; roof tiles might be shaken off; and some columns and beams will probably be cracked. If this occurs during working hours there is a probability of injury." In addition the dome and some beams and columns in the building were vulnerable.

In his report to the Board of Trustees (February 3, 1969), Henry Dreyfuss, chairman of the Buildings and Grounds committee, explained that it might cost as much as $2.5 million to convert the building for revised occupancy and bring it up to seismic standards. Further discussion led to the conclusion that Throop Hall should be demolished, but the question of what to do with the occupants remained unanswered. Two years later the Sylmar earthquake forced the evacuation of the building. The Administrative Offices were moved to the third floor of the Millikan Library, Student Affairs to Dabney Hall of the Humanities, Public Relations to the former Bateman house on San Pasqual Street, and Development to temporary trailers.

Gates Laboratory of Chemistry was also badly damaged in the same earthquake. At first the Buildings and Grounds committee considered demolishing Gates and cutting Throop Hall down to ground level leaving the basement functional. Eventually it was decided to demolish Throop Hall in its entirety, and preserve the existing facade of Gates with a newly constructed interior for use as an Administration building.

Throop Hall, which started out as the center for all academic activities and a gathering place for community events, was demolished in 1973. As a large wrecking ball pounded away at the sturdy walls, mixed emotions circulated among faculty, students and staff. The building, originally named for the city of Pasadena, symbolized Caltech's ancestral home. However, some people welcomed the building's demise. The merits of Hunt and Grey's design had often been questioned, and the interior had been ruined by numerous alterations.

Before Throop Hall was demolished students from Ricketts House salvaged one of its clocks. They suggested to the Board of Trustees that it be installed on Kellogg Laboratory which is where it resides today. The statue of Apollo was moved to Dabney Garden and eventually languished in a storage shed; the Calder arches were cut into pieces and put in a Pasadena storage yard for possible reuse by the City.

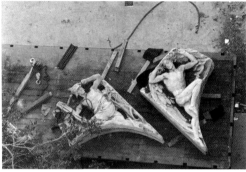

The Calder arches were put in a Pasadena storage yard for possible reuse by the City.

The statue of Apollo was moved to Dabney Garden and eventually languished in a storage shed.

Opposite: Two clocks were added to Throop Hall in 1945. From time to time the clock faces received new identities. This one featured Spiro Agnew. Before the demolition of the building, students from Ricketts House salvaged one of the clocks. After overhauling the motor and providing a surface for the numerals, five of the students made a presentation of the clock to the Board of Trustees. At the students' suggestion it was placed on the north face of Kellogg Laboratory so that it would overlook the Throop site.

Beckman Laboratories of Behavioral Biology. This photo was taken after the closing of San Pasqual Street and the installation of a landscape design created by Land Images. The olive trees were planted as part of Stone's scheme for the approach to the Beckman Auditorium.

Although Alexander may have attempted a uniform architectural style for all the proposed buildings in his plan, different firms interpreted the designs in a variety of ways. Renderings in the Science for Mankind campaign brochure show buildings of reinforced concrete with strong horizontal lines and deeply framed windows. Alexander's contributions are the Baxter Hall of the Humanities and Social Sciences (1971) funded by Mrs. Donald Baxter in memory of her physician husband, and the Beckman Laboratories of Behavioral Biology (1974) funded by the Beckmans. In his design for the Beckman Auditorium, Stone had shown that concrete could be a refined and delicate material. But for the two neighboring structures Alexander used deeply textured surfaces and emphasized the weight and mass of the building's concrete frame. Unfortunately this style, sometimes referred to as "Brutalism," an English term used to describe chunky architecture, overpowers Stone's circular auditorium.

Reinforced concrete is still the dominant material of the South Mudd building (1974)

designed by George Vernon Russell and Associates. But modern interpretations of Mediterranean features: arched windows, implied loggias and circular balconies soften the facade. The Seeley G. Mudd Building of Geophysics and Planetary Science (the division added Planetary Sciences to its name in 1970) was funded primarily by the remainder of Dr. Seeley Mudd's Cypress Mines stock, which had more than doubled in value since being given to Caltech.

Model of Seeley G. Mudd Building of Geophysics and Planetary Science, 1974. In response to a concern that new buildings south of San Pasqual Street should blend with the Goodhue campus, the South Mudd design incorporates Mediterranean features.

CHAPTER TWENTY ONE

The Goldberger Era

"ANY EXPANSION AFTER 1980 SHOULD BE CHANNELED NORTH AS SUGGESTED BY THE ALEXANDER LONG RANGE DEVELOPMENT PLAN OF 1970."

— *Board of Trustees Minutes, June 14, 1974.*

In January, 1977, Harold Brown resigned to become Secretary of Defense to President Carter. Professor Robert F. Christy, who was Vice President and Provost, took over as Acting President until March 1978, when physicist Dr. Marvin Goldberger accepted the Presidency.

Marvin (Murph) Goldberger was born in 1922 in Chicago. After receiving a B.S. in Physics from Carnegie Institute of Technology and a Ph.D. from the University of Chicago, Goldberger served in the U.S. Army for three years. When the war was over he continued with research and teaching in physics before joining the faculty at Princeton where he remained for 21 years. The Inauguration brochure (October 27, 1979) summed up the attributes of Caltech's new President, "Work in theoretical physics and participation in worldwide scientific affairs have won him an international recognition, and he is equally widely known and well regarded as a humanitarian and a dedicated educator, with a singular devotion to undergraduate students."

In January, 1974, Brown had launched a new campaign entitled, "At the Leading Edge." The campaign goal was to raise $130 million over five years. Funding was needed for an engineering center, a gymnasium and graduate housing; a medical sciences program and building; a computer sciences program; and the reconstruction of the Gates Laboratory into an administration building.

The family of Thomas J. Watson, Sr., who had died in 1956 at the age of 82, contributed the major portion of funds for the engineering center. Thomas Watson, who came from a simple farm background, rose to the top of the business community as the founder and head of the IBM Corporation. The family selected Gyo Obata of Hellmuth, Obata and Kassabaum to design the new building, to be called the Thomas J. Watson, Sr. Laboratories of Applied Physics. The building was dedicated on May 5, 1982. Alexander had drawn a rectangular shape flanking the north edge of the mall bordered by Booth, Steele and Keck, but Obata designed a simple square on an axis with Stone's circular auditorium.

Marvin (Murph) Goldberger, President of Caltech from 1978 to 1987. "Among those who know him best, Murph Goldberger is described as considerate, gregarious, and 'down to earth'. He is know to have both sound judgement and a keen sense of humor."

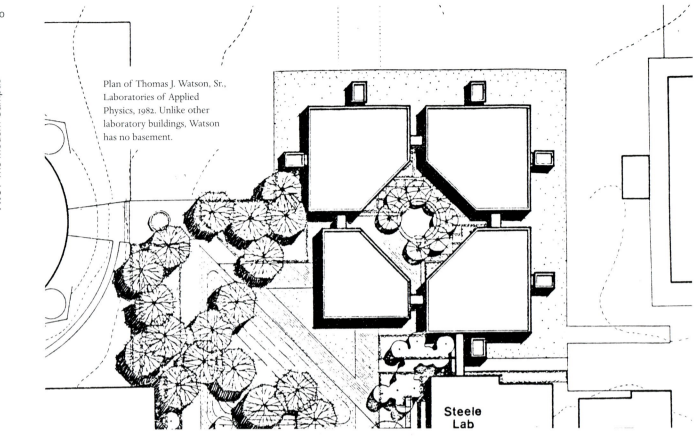

Plan of Thomas J. Watson, Sr., Laboratories of Applied Physics, 1982. Unlike other laboratory buildings, Watson has no basement.

Steele Lab

The square of Watson Laboratory is broken into quadrants whose inner angled walls form a diamond which is a garden courtyard within the outer square. Research laboratories are located on the perimeter and offices face the inner courtyard and central fountain. The main entrance at the southwest corner is set within a sheltering overhang. The design of the building reveals Obata's sensitivity both to the old and the new campus.

In November, 1973, Dr. John Baldeschwieler, chairman of the Chemistry and Chemical Engineering Division, outlined a proposal for a new 85,000 square foot chemistry-biology building to be used primarily for cell biology and cancer research. Seven years later with funds from the Carl F Braun Trust, private donors, and the National Cancer Institute, the building became a reality.

Carl Braun graduated from Stanford in mechanical engineering in 1907. He founded and headed C F Braun and Company, one of the country's leading engineering and construction companies. Braun was a Caltech Associate and Trustee. His company was selected to do the architecture and engineering for the new laboratory. At a meeting of the Buildings and Grounds Committee on December 4, 1978, the representatives of the Braun Corporation explained the design. "The desire to recall some of the attractive features from the older buildings on campus,

The Braun Laboratories were funded and designed by C F Braun and Company. Two residential houses had to be moved to make space for the building. The former Bateman home was moved to Lura street to become offices for a new Environmental Quality Laboratory; the Prufrock house was moved to the west side of Wilson Avenue to become a student residence.

This stone carving of a hand grasping a book was originally installed on Throop Hall under the pilaster representing Law.

was carried out through the tile roof, a red grillwork on part of the sides, red pavers on some covered areas and open walks, and a special treatment of the underside of the overhanging part of the roof."

The Gates Laboratory of Chemistry had stood empty since the 1971 Sylmar earthquake. Eleven years later the Ralph M. Parsons Foundation offered a grant of $1,000,000 to reconstruct it as an administrative center. Additional funds came from the James Irvine Foundation. In 1917, the original laboratory designed by Elmer Grey and Bertram Goodhue had cost $70,000; 66 years later converting a shell into a functional building would cost $2,500,000. The architectural firm of Bobrow/Thomas and Associates (BTA) created a postmodern interior with administrative offices on the second floor and student affairs on the first floor. Caltech's oldest existing structure was reoccupied in the spring of 1983. Michael Bobrow, chairman of BTA said about the restoration, "Caltech has made an important statement about its rich heritage by giving new life to the Gates Laboratory." In addition to honoring Ralph M. Parsons, the original donors' names were retained in the new designation, the Parsons-Gates Hall of Administration.

In 1986 Arnold and Mabel Beckman provided funds for a new laboratory for research in bio-organic chemistry, polymers, natural product synthesis and catalysis. Parts of Crellin and Church were renovated to form the 33,000 square foot Beckman Laboratory of Chemical Synthesis. Robert Fort, director of Physical Plant and members of his staff decided that by enlarging a bridge, which connected the two buildings, the Calder sculptures from Throop Hall could be incorporated into the laboratory's north facade.

Three Presidents, three fund raising campaigns and two modern master plans had created the buildings that kept Caltech in the forefront of scientific research. But the campus, which was now more than double its original size, was no longer the unified architectural masterpiece which Hale had envisioned. Fortunately a landscaping program, organized and funded by Stephen Bechtel, chairman of the Buildings and Grounds Committee, helped establish a much needed cohesiveness to a disparate campus. In addition several projects had introduced a nostalgia for features of the early campus: the return of the Calder Arches; Obata's creation of an interior courtyard with pool and fountain; and the Braun Corporation's use of a tile roof and terra-cotta grillwork.

ARNOLD AND MABEL BECKMAN
LABORATORY OF CHEMICAL SYNTHESIS

The Arnold and Mabel Beckman Laboratory of Chemical Synthesis, 1986. After careful restoration and some recasting, the Calder sculptures were installed over arched windows, similar to Throop's entrance. The two end pilasters and their plaques were installed on free-standing pillars in the courtyard behind because there was insufficient space for them where the bridge abuts Crellin and Church. The two center plaques, a mask representing The Arts and a hammer and anvil representing Science, were mistakenly reversed on Throop Hall and are now in their correct positions.

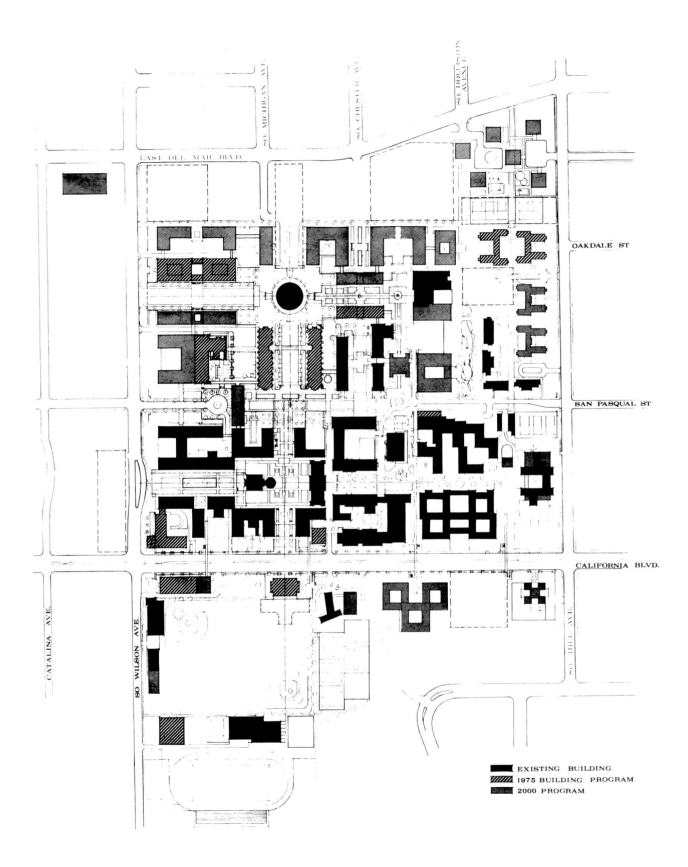

1975–2000 Long Range
Development Plan.

CHAPTER TWENTY TWO

The 1989 Master Plan

"THE MASTER PLAN ADDRESSES FOUR PRIMARY OBJECTIVES: TO PROVIDE FOR THE FUTURE GROWTH OF CALTECH'S ACADEMIC DIVISIONS; TO PROVIDE AN APPROPRIATE INTERFACE BETWEEN THE CAMPUS AND SURROUNDING RESIDENTIAL NEIGHBORHOODS; TO MINIMIZE UNCERTAINTY ABOUT CALTECH'S FUTURE DEVELOPMENT ON THE PART OF ITS NEIGHBORS AND THE CITY OF PASADENA AND AT THE SAME TIME STREAMLINE DEVELOPMENT PROCEDURES; AND TO PROVIDE A UNIFIED, BALANCED, AND ATTRACTIVE PLAN FOR FUTURE GROWTH."

— *Master Plan Report, July, 1989*

In 1987, Thomas E. Everhart, whose training is in engineering, was chosen as the first non physicist to become President of Caltech. Everhart was born in 1932 in Kansas City, Missouri. After receiving an undergraduate degree at Harvard College, he went on to earn a M.Sc. at UCLA and a Ph.D. from Cambridge University in England. Prior to accepting the Caltech position, Everhart had been chancellor at the Urbana-Champaign campus of the University of Illinois. He is a recognized national spokesman on science and technology.

During Everhart's tenure as president, plans for the campus expansion to Del Mar were settled and six building projects were completed. However, before this successful program was launched the previous administration had faced a new challenge.

In July 1985, the City of Pasadena changed its zoning ordinances and adopted new codes. According to the Institute's report, "nonprofit institutions occupying two or more acres and planning 5,000 square feet or more of future construction were advised to submit a Master Development Plan to the City for review and approval." Caltech's previous Master Plans were used for internal planning only and had not been subject to city review.

In 1986, Meyer & Allen Associates (formerly Kurt Meyer Partners), specialists in civic and institutional architecture and campus planning, were hired to develop "the most comprehensive plan ever outlined for the physical development of the campus." The plan included an Environmental Impact Report, and a study on traffic flow and parking. The final approved plan was subject to review every five years.

A fifteen year estimate of the campus population (to the year 2000) showed that the Institute had no plan to change its undergraduate enrollment. However the rate of increase per year for the faculty and support staff was estimated at 1%, and for the graduate students up to 1.4%. With the present enrollment of about 2,000 graduate and undergraduate students, visitors often wonder why the campus is so large. Land is

Thomas E. Everhart, President of Caltech from 1987 to 1997. Everhart, whose training is in engineering, broke the sequence of physicists who had headed the Institute.

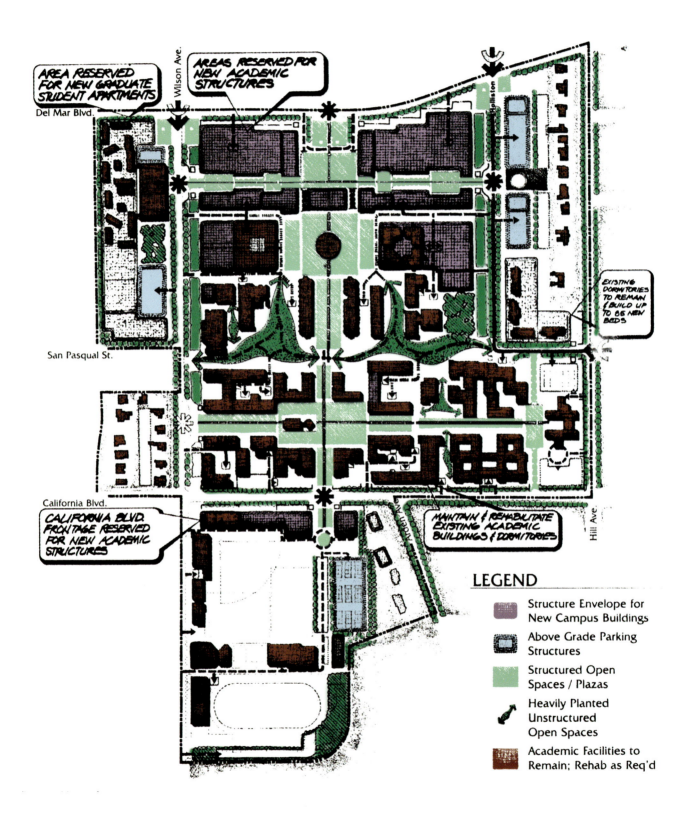

AREA RESERVED FOR NEW GRADUATE STUDENT APARTMENTS

Wilson Ave.

AREAS RESERVED FOR NEW ACADEMIC STRUCTURES

Holliston

Del Mar Blvd.

EXISTING DORMITORIES TO REMAIN & BUILD UP TO 85 NEW BEDS

San Pasqual St.

California Blvd.

CALIFORNIA BLVD. FRONTAGE RESERVED FOR NEW ACADEMIC STRUCTURES

Wilson

MAINTAIN & REHABILITATE EXISTING ACADEMIC BUILDINGS & DORMITORIES

Hill Ave.

LEGEND

Structure Envelope for New Campus Buildings

Above Grade Parking Structures

Structured Open Spaces / Plazas

Heavily Planted Unstructured Open Spaces

Academic Facilities to Remain; Rehab as Req'd

needed for new laboratories and scientific equipment.

The academic areas of the north campus were to be divided into two parts with biology and chemistry in the northwest section, and chemical engineering, engineering and applied science in the northeast area. Physics, mathematics, astronomy and the geological and planetary science buildings would create a frontage along California Boulevard, east of Wilson Avenue. Student housing expansion would continue on the east side of campus toward Del Mar Boulevard, with graduate student housing on the western border. Athletic facilities would remain on the south side of California Boulevard.

Clifton Allen, the partner in charge of the project, stressed the importance of returning to the structure and organization of the Goodhue campus. The Pereira-Luckman and Alexander plans disregarded the spirit of the early campus with its defining east-west axis, the integration of landscape and architecture, and the concept of a unified plan. Instead isolated cubes were placed on a north-south orientation to maximize the mountain views and face existing streets which might become malls or pathways in the future.

Caltech's new Master Plan required by the City of Pasadena. The plan called for a 124-acre campus bordered by Catalina Avenue on the west, Hill Avenue on the east, Del Mar Boulevard on the north, California Boulevard on the south, and an area south of California Boulevard between Arden Road and Wilson Avenue.

In the 1989 plan, axes would be expanded and reinforced. The north-south axis which terminated at the Beckman Auditorium in the Alexander Plan would extend to Del Mar Boulevard, with a gateway to identify a major entrance. As new buildings would be constructed the entrance into the athletic facilities on the south side of California would be aligned with Goodhue's original courtyard entrance between East Bridge and Sloan buildings. A secondary east-west axis running from Holliston Avenue to Wilson Avenue, was moved further north to align with Lura Street. Thus the main axes would create an H-shaped circulation pattern to help visitors understand the geography, and to repeat the orientation of the Goodhue plan. The San Pasqual pathway would remain as a free form design because the buildings are orientated in both directions. In keeping with Goodhue's east-west demarcation, the new North Mall was to feature domed porches and bordering arcades alternating with plazas. Additional domed porches were suggested as identification for campus entrances on the north-south axis.

The parklike setting, which was established by Goodhue's scheme at the request of Caltech's original leaders, and redirected under the guidance of Stephen Bechtel, was to be enhanced by courtyards, fountains and imaginative landscaping. To strengthen the importance of the Del Mar gateway and make it a window into the campus, a raised plaza above underground parking was to be set between a landscaped forecourt and the east-west axis. The plan stated that buildings aligning the plaza may be oriented north-south, and a taller building to be sited south of the plaza might have a multi-story open atrium to retain visibility of Beckman Auditorium. Goodhue used walls and arbors to protect the scholarly calm of his campus from the intrusions of the surrounding city. In a similar way, the edges of the expanded campus would have walls modeled on those of Goodhue and Kaufmann.

In addition to complying with the City's restrictions, the Master Plan also addressed the impact of the campus community on the surrounding neighborhoods. Home-owners expressed concern over large buildings, traffic circulation, parking, noise and intrusive lighting. By remaining residential in character, the edges of the campus would serve as buffers. The new plan left the offices (in former residences) on Wilson and Hill Avenues in place while some Arden Road properties were to be renovated, and others would be replaced by vintage houses from Holliston Avenue. Historic Tournament Park was to be preserved to screen the Athletic facilities from the nearby houses. Graduate student housing on Catalina Avenue was to be no higher than three stories.

The plan stipulated that before an existing house could be demolished it must be offered to any resident who could relocate it. A financial supplement and assistance was included in the relocation package. The historic Tolman-Bacher house on the corner of Michigan Avenue and Lura Street could not be moved for 15 years.

To accommodate more cars in less surface space, two parking structures were located on Holliston Avenue and two on the west side of Wilson Avenue. Underground lots were planned under new tennis courts south of California Boulevard, under the Athenaeum tennis courts, and between Del Mar and the Beckman Auditorium. Some existing surface lots were to remain.

Although the Master Plan report does not stipulate a specific architectural style for the North Campus, it does explain that Goodhue's academic buildings and Kaufmann's residential complex were designed not as individual statements but as unified schemes. The report suggests that the "attitude" of the original buildings "should be a guiding principle."

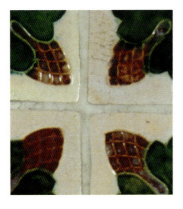

CHAPTER TWENTY THREE

The North Campus

BECKMAN INSTITUTE

"SINCE CALTECH'S NEWER BUILDINGS AROUND THE BECKMAN AUDITORIUM REPRESENT A VARIETY OF STYLES, INFILL DEVELOPMENT BETWEEN THE ORIGINAL CAMPUS AND THE NEW EAST-WEST MALL NEED NOT NECESSARILY BE CONSTRAINED IN ARCHITECTURAL STYLE, THOUGH NEW BUILDINGS IN THIS AREA COULD SET THE TONE FOR THE REMAINDER OF DEVELOPMENT TO THE NORTH."

— *Master Plan Report 1989*

The 1989 Beckman Institute, which was designed as a center for integrated research in the chemical and biological sciences, was the first building of the new Master Plan. Once again Arnold and Mabel Beckman had given Caltech an extraordinary gift. In keeping with Beckman's own work, the mission of the new laboratory is "to foster the invention of methods, materials, and instrumentation that will open new avenues of scientific investigation in biology, chemistry and related sciences."

Albert C. Martin and Associates were selected in an informal design competition as the architects for the project. Three generations of Martins established the firm's place in the architectural history of Los Angeles. Albert C. Martin, Sr, founded the business in 1906. Like his contemporary, Bertram Goodhue, Martin used Churrigueresque decoration for some of his earlier buildings. But his 1928 collaborative design for the Los Angeles City Hall is more in keeping with Goodhue's central library. Designs executed by the present generation of Martins range from sleek steel and glass towers for the Union Bank and Atlantic Richfield plazas to a Gothic-inspired Home Savings of America.

The circular Beckman Auditorium was now aligned with the square-shaped Watson Laboratories on the east side, and the rectangular-shaped Beckman Institute on the west side. At this key site the new laboratory building served as a transition between the middle modern campus and the new north campus. Following the guidelines of the new Master Plan, Project Designer Tim Vreeland took inspirations from the Goodhue and Kaufmann buildings thus setting the tone for the North Campus area.

The Beckman Institute's 163,000 square feet seems mammoth compared to laboratory buildings of Goodhue's campus. However, the massing of the building is lightened by a central courtyard and arcades which are similar to Goodhue's portales. Laboratories, which require high ceilings and a heavier floor load, are housed in the two-story north and south wings. An eleven

Beckman Institute, 1989. A long reflecting pool unites Arnold Beckman's two greatest gifts to Caltech, the Auditorium and the Biology-Chemistry Institute.

A shell motif marks the center of the building. Shells are typical motifs of Renaissance architecture. Goodhue used them in his Churrigueresque decorations on the early campus buildings.

Simple decorative elements were used to strengthen the building's relationship to the early campus. A large, abstracted shell focusses the eye on the center of the building; stylized acanthus leaves adorn the tops of shallow piers; overlapping scallop shapes, reminiscent of Goodhue's lambrequins, flow down the sides of the massive corner columns; a broken pediment surmounted by Caltech's symbol, the torch of knowledge, identifies stairwells in the north and south wings.

Exterior double stairways, modeled on the central courtyard of Kaufmann's dormitories, provide easy access to seating areas below. Each area forms a different geometric shape and was designed as a place for unplanned encounters or relaxation. The main entry hall at the north-east corner is decorated with tilework using motifs copied from some of Goodhue's buildings.

foot-high parapet, broken by small attic windows similar to the Parsons-Gates building, hides fume hoods and exhaust ducts. A three-story office section with a red tile roof, reflects the residential style of Kaufmann's Athenaeum and forms a bridge between the laboratory wings.

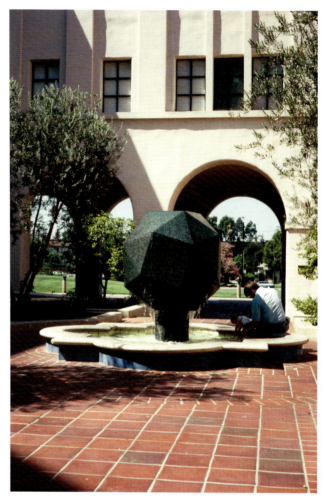

A broken pediment over Beckman Institute's stairwell windows was inspired by a similar design over the Olive Walk entrance to Fleming House. According to Project Designer, Tim Vreeland, the curved shape represents the wings of Pegasus, symbol of poetic inspiration.

Top Right: Water flows over a polyhedron-shaped granite block into a Moorish-inspired quatrefoil basin.

Goodhue's sketch for the courtyard of his proposed Science Museum shows a fountain in the center of a quatrefoil-shaped basin. This could have been the inspiration for the Beckman Institute courtyard.

VIEW IN SCIENCE MVSEVM COVRT·LOOKING NORTH WEST·

The Moore Laboratory of Engineering

Tympanums above the windows on the north facing wings feature an integrated circuit (computer chip) on one side and microwave parabolic antennas on the other. The design of the computer chip (picture shown) has one less "pad" on the left side. Did the artist do this intentionally to release the evil spirits?

"The Moore Laboratory will reinforce the intellectual and architectural bridge between biology and engineering begun when the Beckman Institute was constructed on campus."
— *Dedication Program, January 9, 1996*

Gordon and Betty Moore Laboratory of Engineering, 1996. The front of the building is U-shaped and with its arcades forms one of the borders of the new North Mall.

The Moore Laboratory of Engineering was dedicated on January 9, 1996. Situated to the northeast of Beckman Auditorium, it is the first building to flank one side of the new North Mall. Through the generosity of Gordon and Betty Moore, this "unique, state-of-the-art center...will help shape the computing and communication industries of the 21st century."

Gordon Moore was born in San Francisco. He graduated from the University of California at Berkeley and received a Ph.D. in chemistry from Caltech in 1954. He cofounded Intel Corporation in 1968 to develop and produce large scale integrated products. He joined Caltech's Board of Trustees in 1983 and became its chairman in 1994. Gordon and Betty Moore are life members of The Caltech Associates and the President's Circle, and have endowed a professorship in engineering and an undergraduate scholarship.

Neptune Thomas Davis, an architectural firm experienced in campus planning and design, was selected for the project. As Neptune, Thomas and Associates they designed the Booth Computing Center in 1963 and Downs and Lauritsen Laboratories in 1969.

For buildings bordering his east-west mall, Goodhue created continuous fronts connected to arcades to strengthen the urban context and sense of uniformity. The backs of the buildings opened onto courtyards to allow for future expansion. In contrast to Goodhue's frontage, the Moore Laboratory has a plain facade in the rear with two wings around a courtyard facing the North Mall. Tony O'Keefe, the partner in charge of the project, explained that the C-shaped design was done to create as many windows as possible, to orient the building towards the new north campus, and to be consistent with the design of the Beckman Institute.

A rough stucco finish camouflages a concrete shell constructed at 50% over seismic code requirements. With three levels above ground and two below, the building includes a floor of teaching laboratories and two lecture halls. Ceiling and lighting treatments in the corridors incorporate a trough to carry

Fountain in the entrance courtyard. The patterns in the tiles are symbolic representations of an analog integrated circuit developed in the computation and neural systems laboratory of Professor Carver Mead. The tiles were designed by Kwabena Boahen, a graduate student in Mead's group, and Jim Campbell, a staff engineer. Campbell explained that the design was inspired by Professor Mark Konishi's research exploring how the owl uses hearing to locate its prey.

computer cables which can be accessed and changed with ease. Red tiles cover the roof of the center section, and with the exception of spindly antennas and microwave dishes all the mechanical equipment is hidden by a high parapet over the wings.

In keeping with the Goodhue Associates' buildings of the West Court, restrained decoration reflects the scientific work of the laboratory. According to the dedication brochure, "Investigators in the Moore Laboratory are certain to make discoveries in science and engineering of significant benefit to industry and to humankind."

Opposite: A Romanesque-style doorway identifies the main entrance.

Avery House

"Avery House will be a living legacy of Stan's entrepreneurial spirit that will benefit future generations of Caltech students, faculty, and staff."

— *Invitation to the Groundbreaking Ceremony, May 9, 1995*

The Master Plan was to provide on campus housing for 100% of the undergraduate student body and 50% to 60% of the graduate student body. When the first draft of the Master Plan was drawn up in 1989, additional undergraduate dormitories were to be built behind the existing graduate houses on the corner of Holliston Avenue and San Pasqual Street. In 1995, this scheme was dropped and a separate complex was planned for the southwest corner of Del Mar Boulevard and Holliston Avenue.

To encourage greater interaction outside of the classroom between faculty, graduates and undergraduates, a scheme for a mixed housing facility was devised. Although the new location would place the undergraduates further away from the main campus dormitories, the building would create an anchor for the northeast corner, and become a border for the North Mall.

Originally named "Centennial House," the project was renamed for Stan Avery who generously gave $10 million for its construction. R. Stanton Avery was born in Oklahoma and earned a bachelor's degree from Pomona College. In 1932 he invented self-adhesive labels. From a modest beginning the business grew into the world-wide multibillion-dollar Avery Dennison Corporation.

Avery joined Caltech's Board of Trustees in 1971, and served as chairman between 1974 and 1985. He endowed a professorship and established the Avery Endowment Fund. Members of the Caltech community have also benefited from the Durfee Foundation which Avery created to provide funds for travel and study in China.

Santa Monica architects Moore Ruble Yudell were chosen to design the building. The late Charles Moore designed Kresge College at UC Santa Cruz, John Ruble worked on research facilities for UC San Diego and the University of Washington, and Buzz Yudell was responsible for four new science buildings at the University of Oregon, as well as the Plaza Las Fuentes in Pasadena.

Principal-in-charge, Buzz Yudell, looked to the early campus for inspiration, and modeled the layout of Avery House's 80,000 square feet on Kaufmann's South Student Houses. Although Avery House is not divided into individual houses, buildings and walls define courtyards with entrances to groups of rooms from different locations. The main courtyard facing south is a communal gathering place and is used for campus functions. A wrought-iron fence and locked gate protect the inner living areas. A library, which houses memorabilia of Stan Avery's career, doubles for meetings or private dining.

Double rooms with bunk beds and modular furniture accommodate 140 students. Five faculty apartments, one at each corner

Avery House, 1996. The architecture of this residential complex was inspired by Kaufmann's dormitories. The Mediteranean theme is reinforced by the use of stucco walls, red tile roofs, arcades and colorful tile work. Inner and outer towers define corners and give variety to the roof lines.

An outer south-facing courtyard serves as a common area with outside and inside gathering spaces, food service, and a large two-story dining hall with a trussed ceiling.

Arcades bordering the North Mall have rectangular piers and follow the form of Goodhue's portales. The arcades around the communal courtyard have round columns and resemble Kaufmann's designs.

and one in the center, have their own entry, garden court and space for parking. Small dining rooms, common rooms, kitchens and informal meeting rooms are scattered throughout the houses.

Visitors, seminars and a special library aimed to teach and encourage entrepreneurship are an integral part of life at Avery House. Stan Avery, who died in 1997 a year after celebrating the opening of his dormitory, "provided the resources to make Avery House one of the most innovative dormitories in America — to wit, a dorm with an entrepreneurial focus that would both celebrate and support the spirit of innovation and invention."

Tile work in the arcades with the motto, "Creativity, Tenacity, Integrity." This triangular logo defines the qualities of Stan Avery and a philosophy for Avery House.

CHAPTER TWENTY FOUR

The South Campus

"The opportunity for this priceless addition to the Institute's facilities for developing robust and strong limbed men will soon be gone, and it should be used at once."

— *Robert A. Millikan, 1922*

At a meeting of the Board of Trustees on March 10, 1922, Millikan stressed the need for 6 or 8 acres separate to the main 22-acre campus for athletic facilities and a gym. The cost was estimated at $40,000. Since 1910 students had used a park on the south side of California Boulevard for their playing fields. The City-owned area had been home of the original Tournament of Roses game.

In 1937, it was announced in the *Pasadena Star News* that "The long-talked-of Caltech gymnasium, sidetracked many times in the ambitious campus developments during the past ten years, is brought into the open once more through action of a representative alumni committee." Michael C. Brunner '25 was leading the campaign to raise $250,000 for a building at the southwest corner of California Boulevard and Arden Road,

A 1922 photograph of Tournament Park showing a trolley car on California Boulevard. With the growing popularity of football the Tournament of Roses Association realized that the 25,000 capacity bleachers were inadequate. In the early 1920s they raised funds to build the Rose Bowl and the city leased Tournament Park to Caltech.

Rendering of Braun Athletic Center, 1992. A horizontal cornice accentuates the roof line and an arcaded facade identifies the main entrance.

backing up to Tournament Park. Plans for a three-story structure and outdoor swimming pool were prepared by Gordon Kaufmann. The building would include a basketball floor with bleachers and gallery, lockers, wrestling, boxing, and fencing accommodations, and offices for doctors and coaches. Unfortunately the building never materialized. Perhaps funding was never received or the Institute was preoccupied with the establishment of its scientific buildings.

In 1947, during the DuBridge era, "the voters of Pasadena approved abandonment of Tournament Park and its sale to the Institute" with the proviso that a small area be retained as a neighborhood park. Caltech students had the use of a baseball diamond, tennis courts, dirt volleyball and basketball courts, and Paddock Field, a football field and track named in honor of Charlie Paddock, Pasadena's greatest athlete. But for more than 40 years athletes had managed

with out-of-date dressing rooms and no locker rooms. They had to shower at their dorms or at the Throop Club.

It took another seven years before the previously planned Athletic Center, now consisting of a gym, swimming pool, outdoor playing courts and parking, was constructed. Instead of the corner of California Boulevard and Arden Road, the building was located further south and a Student Union, which was to have been part of the original complex, was relocated on the main campus. The Alumni paid for the swimming pool and the Scott Brown Trust paid for the gymnasium. Ignoring Kaufmann's 1930s design, Pereira and Luckman created schematic designs for a contemporary building. In 1954 the architectural firm of Marsh, Smith and Powell completed a modern structure with an arched roof supported by concrete buttresses.

Braun Athletic Center has
a spacious lobby with a
circular reception desk.
The two-story space is
now home to the statue of
Apollo which used to
grace the main staircase of
Throop Hall.

Tennis Court / Parking Structure

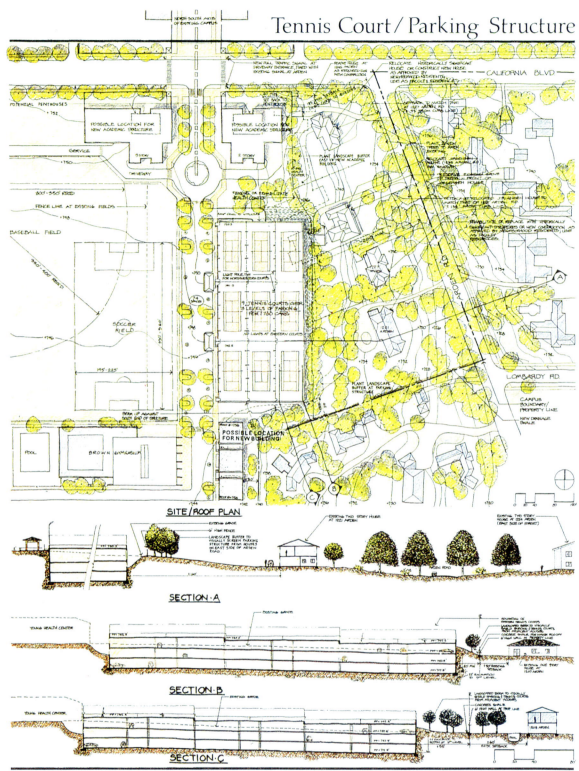

SITE/ROOF PLAN

SECTION · A

SECTION · B

SECTION · C

CALIFORNIA INSTITUTE OF TECHNOLOGY   MASTER PLAN

KURT MEYER PARTNERS

JULY 1995

The 1989 Master Plan explained that, with the exception of the proposed academic buildings facing California Boulevard, the 1986 Morrisroe Astroscience Laboratory and the Central Plant Cooling Towers and Cogeneration buildings facing Wilson Avenue, the South Campus would be devoted to athletic facilities.

In 1984 the Carl F Braun Trust (which had already given Caltech a building for Chemistry and Biology) funded a second swimming pool, an expansion of the 1954 Scott Brown Gymnasium and an upgrade of the existing locker rooms. A few years later the same family generously gave $4.7 million as part of "The Campaign for Caltech" to build a two-story gymnasium at the west end of the swimming pools on Wilson Avenue.

In 1992 the 42,000 square foot Braun Athletic Center opened. O. K. Earl Corporation, who designed several buildings on campus including the previous athletic additons, designed a simple building in the spirit of the early campus. Facilities include a main gym, a dance/aerobic room and a weight room with state-of-the-art equipment. Six racquetball/squash courts, which had been planned for a separate structure, were integrated into the building.

The two-story lobby is now home to Caltech's much loved Apollo, god of sunlight, prophecy, music and healing. He was acquired for Throop Hall in 1910 by Elmer Grey. For many years the statue had been forgotten. Moved from one storage space to another it had lost some of its appendages and been the object of pseudo-artistic decoration. Attempts to find a new home for the god failed until the 1990s. After learning that Apollo might end up in a dumpster, Tom Lehman of Public Events urged Professor Robert Rosenstone, head of the Institute's art committee, to save the statue.

To preserve the marble, conservation experts advised an interior setting. With the enthusiastic support of Dan Bridges, recently retired Director of Athletics, the lobby of the Braun Athletic Center was chosen. John Griswold of Griswold Conservation Associates was in charge of the restoration. He made a replica of the statue's "private parts" from photographs of the original Apollo Belvedere in the Vatican, and he recast and re-attached lost fingers. He also cleaned the marble and reduced iron stains. But graffiti on eyes, lips, eyebrows and other areas made by blue marking pens and colored nail polish proved impossible to remove, and has been covered with a special coating. Alumni will welcome back their Apollo statue with enthusiasm, and Rosenstone hopes that visitors to the gym will improve their appreciation of art.

Opposite: Future Development of the Athletic Area. To complete the improvements to Caltech's athletic facilities, the playing fields will expand approximately 80 feet to the east when the driveway from California Boulevard is relocated to align with the north-south axis. After the planned underground parking lot is built new tennis courts will be constructed on top. Additional landscaping will shield the courts and the parking from Arden Road neighbors, and the playing fields will be hidden from California Boulevard by academic buildings.

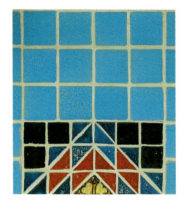

CHAPTER TWENTY FIVE

Infills and Renovations

THE SHERMAN FAIRCHILD LIBRARY

"ANY PHYSICAL CHANGES OR ADDITIONS WITHIN THE ORIGINAL CAMPUS SHOULD BE SYMPATHETIC TO AND COMPATIBLE WITH THE SCALE AND ARCHITECTURAL STYLE OF CALTECH'S ORIGINAL BUILDINGS."

— *Master Plan Report, 1989*

Since 1967 when a new central plant was constructed on Wilson Avenue, south of California Boulevard, the Goodhue Associates 1925 Steam Plant and Chemical Engineering Laboratory, located between Thomas and Spalding Engineering buildings, had been degraded to a catch-all storage facility. In 1995, as part of the Campaign for Caltech the Sherman Fairchild Foundation contributed $9.63 million for the construction of an engineering and applied science library to replace the 1925 building.

Sherman Fairchild was a pioneer in the fields of photography, aviation, and sound engineering. He founded the Fairchild Camera & Instrument Corporation and the Fairchild Engine and Airplane Corporation. He is described as "an astute businessman ...and a voracious reader who subscribed regularly to 150 trade and technical journals." The Fairchild Foundation has also sponsored the Sherman Fairchild Distinguished Scholars Program and the Sherman Fairchild Postdoctoral Scholars in Physics, Mathematics and Astronomy. Foundation President Walter Burke has been on Caltech's Board of Trustees since 1975.

Situated in the heart of the engineering facilities on campus, the new library consolidated seven libraries in engineering and applied science which had been scattered around campus in various locations including Millikan Library. Most of the branch libraries will become reading rooms electronically connected to the new library. The center contains the latest information retrieval systems and communications technology. Every table is wired with fiber optic cabling enabling complete access to the campus computer network system.

Architects Moore Ruble Yudell found the constraints of the physical space between the two existing buildings challenging. But with horizontal molding defining the base and cornice, the building aligns perfectly with its neighbors making it hard to believe it was constructed nearly half a century later. The 35,854 square foot space consists of three floors above ground and two below. For now the second basement is assigned to chemical engineering and is not accessible from the library.

In spite of its focus on technology the building has been designed to create the kind of warm environment associated with a classic library. Elements from the Goodhue and Kaufmann designs have been successfully integrated. An arched doorway defines the main entrance and the hipped red tile roof is consistent with the nearby wing of Dabney Hall.

The library's interior is divided into two parts. The core area is devoted to offices, meeting rooms, a multimedia conference room, specialized computer workstations, and copying facilities, grouped around an open staircase. The second area consists of the main reference section, stacks and a reading room. Stone stairs, interrupted by wood benches at each landing, lead to a magnificent, barrel vaulted reading room modeled on the Linonia and Brothers room at Yale.

A set of bronze interlocking gears, placed on the inside of a small balcony outside the third floor reading room, is the only memento that remains of the demolished Steam Plant and Chemical Engineering Laboratory.

Sherman Fairchild Library of Engineering and Applied Science, 1997. A recessed patio and stepped garden court on one side and a view of the secluded Dabney garden on the other recall Goodhue's aim to integrate landscape and architecture.

Opposite: West entrance to the Fairchild Library. An arched doorway framed by art-deco light fixtures, which resemble stacked books, defines this entrance and contrasts with the horizontal lines of the facade.

Fairchild Library's third floor reading room. A barrel vaulted wood paneled ceiling dominates a room furnished with Craftsman-style cherry wood tables and chairs, copper reading lamps, groupings of lounge chairs and a half circle alcove with bench. Clerestory windows and soft ambiant lighting complete the setting.

Winnett Center Renovation

Winnett Student Center was enlarged and renovated in 1998. To blend the center with the early campus, design elements from Kaufman"s student dormitories were incorporated. A new south facade features a rescaled copy of Kaufmann's arcades, including new casts of some of the capital faces originally made by alumnus John Hood.

The Winnett Student Center was constructed in 1962 with funds provided by P. G. Winnett, a Pasadena resident, owner of the Bullocks Department Store and a member of Caltech's Board of Trustees. It took the place of Caltech's original temporary dormitory known as "The Old Dorm," and provided space for a bookstore, central lounge, meeting rooms and headquarters for student clubs.

By the late 1990s the bookstore needed more space in order to adequately serve a modern scientific institution. As part of the enlargement scheme a new exterior was constructed. AC Martin Partners, (formerly Albert C. Martin and Associates) who had designed the Beckman Institute, were hired for the project.

The student center is an important component of the residential section of campus which contains Kaufmann's 1931 South Student Houses, the three north dormitories and Chandler Dining Hall built in 1960. In keeping with the guidelines of the 1989 Master Plan, Kaufmann's architecture was used as a prototype. After careful studies of his buildings, which were influenced by the architecture of Andalusia, selected elements

The wall of named bricks which had come from the fireplace of the original Throop Club stayed in place but was recessed behind the new arcade. The opposite side of the wall, in which additional bricks are set, is now visible from inside the bookstore.

were incorporated into the new design of Winnett, including arcades and capitals featuring characters who represent student life.

The wall of bricks from the original Throop Club fireplace remained undisturbed, and customers entering the renovated bookstore can step over the fireplace's brass "T". Inside, a colorful tile floor leads into a spacious store with well-organized book shelves, displays of Caltech-related memorabilia, a separate computer shop, and seating areas with large leather armchairs. A door to the north leads into the Red Door Cafe. On the upper level there are enlarged meeting rooms and lounges, an outdoor deck with its own staircase, and a remodeled Radio Club office. Landscaping and patios with outdoor furniture link Winnett to Chandler, and create a typical California setting for student gatherings and dining.

AC Martin's redesign of Winnett has produced a more viable student center. The 1960s plain box now blends with the early campus architecture "to create the collegial environment sought after by Caltech."

Caltech's beaver guards the bookstore's main doorway. This bas relief was executed for the 1962 Winnett Center by Albert Stewart, a world renowned sculptor known for his animal subjects. He also designed the bronze plaque for the Thomas Hunt Morgan memorial in the Biology library.

CHAPTER TWENTY SIX

Open Spaces

"[OUR AIM IS] TO INCREASE COHESIVENESS AND ATMOSPHERE OF THE CAMPUS, PERHAPS THROUGH LANDSCAPING AND OTHER MEANS, WITH A GOAL OF CONVEYING A FEELING OF A MORE UNIFIED CAMPUS."
— *Stephen Bechtel, chairman of Buildings and Grounds Committee, October 29, 1978*

CAMPUS BEAUTIFICATION

In spite of Beatrix Farrand's insistence on a master landscaping plan, only a few separate areas of the original campus were professionally designed. After 1945, the rapid growth of the postwar era left little time or money for a professional scheme to treat the open spaces.

Following the demolition of Caltech's first building in 1973, the students suggested a garden in place of the formal concrete stairway proposed by A. Quincy Jones, architect for the Throop Study. Jones redesigned the area with winding paths following a sloping bank, ponds, water cascades, rocks, trees and shrubs.

On August 1, 1978, the Buildings and Grounds Committee, with Stephen D. Bechtel as chairman, met and suggested a review of the long range plans for the campus growth. Bechtel "indicated he hoped the Committee could suggest ways to increase the architectural cohesiveness of the campus, to provide the feeling that the campus is a more unified entity...but there is no intention of modifying the exterior of the

Throop Gardens, circa 1975. At the suggestion of the students the site of Throop Hall was designed as an inviting garden with trees, shrubs and cascading pools. The Cleveland Wrecking Company donated a stately cedar deodar to replace the Christmas tree it had to remove from the dome of Throop Hall during the demolition process.

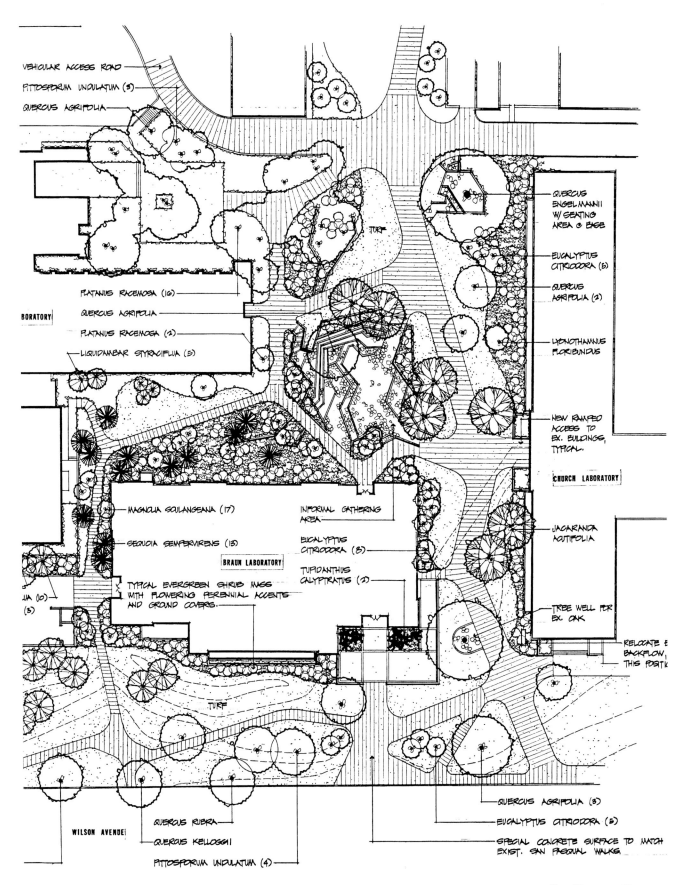

VEHICULAR ACCESS ROAD
PITTOSPORUM UNDULATUM (3)
QUERCUS AGRIFOLIA

QUERCUS ENGELMANNII W/ SEATING AREA @ BASE
EUCALYPTUS CITRIODORA (5)
QUERCUS AGRIFOLIA (2)
LYONOTHAMNUS FLORIBUNDUS
NEW RAMPED ACCESS TO EX. BUILDINGS, TYPICAL.

TURF

PLATANUS RACEMOSA (10)
QUERCUS AGRIFOLIA
PLATANUS RACEMOSA (2)
LIQUIDAMBAR STYRACIFLUA (5)

BORATORY

CHURCH LABORATORY

MAGNOLIA SOULANGEANA (17)
SEQUOIA SEMPERVIRENS (15)

BRAUN LABORATORY

TYPICAL EVERGREEN SHRUB MASS WITH FLOWERING PERENNIAL ACCENTS AND GROUND COVERS.

INFORMAL GATHERING AREA
EUCALYPTUS CITRIODORA (3)
TUPIDANTHUS CALYPTRATUS (2)

JACARANDA ACUTIFOLIA

TREE WELL FOR EX. OAK

UA (10)
(3)

RELOCATE & BACKFLOW, THIS POSITN

TURF

WILSON AVENUE

QUERCUS RUBRA
QUERCUS KELLOGGII
PITTOSPORUM UNDULATUM (4)

QUERCUS AGRIFOLIA (3)
EUCALYPTUS CITRIODORA (5)
SPECIAL CONCRETE SURFACE TO MATCH EXIST. SAN PASQUAL WALKS.

SAN PASQUAL PATHWAY

Landscaping plans by Land Images for the San Pasqual pathway near the Braun laboratory, and the Bechtel Mall between Wilson Avenue and the Millikan Library.

buildings themselves or dictating a uniform architectural style for future buildings."

Bechtel is Chairman Emeritus of Bechtel Group Inc., a worldwide engineering and construction business, and The Fremont Group and Sequoia Ventures Inc., separate affiliated companies operating in real estate, natural resources and related fields.

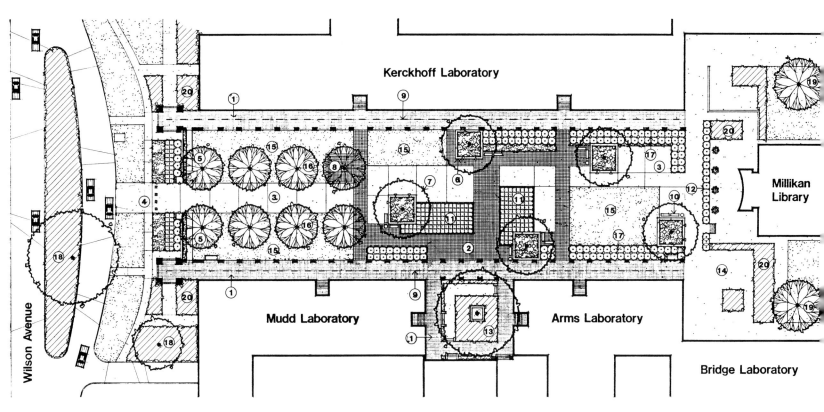

BECHTEL MALL

An oak tree with seating area for quiet study along the San Pasqual pathway.

Landscaping became the key to Bechtel's push for a campus cohesiveness. Thomas A. Lockett, principal of the firm Land Images, which has been in charge of Caltech's landscape architecture since 1975, found that the campus lacked green space, color, signage, and seating areas for small gatherings or quiet study. There was also a need to integrate separate sections of the grounds into a more unified setting.

The Goodhue campus plan saw the landscape as a response to the architecture which was supposed to define, control and contain the area. Changes were made cautiously. Dabney garden was renovated but Farrand's traditional design respected; the south entry to the Athenaeum was improved; the Olive Walk which defined the east-west pathway was paved in red brick with grassy areas planted on either side. Later, the area between the Thomas and Guggenheim laboratories was redesigned. Elm trees killed by beetles were replaced by deciduous Tipu trees which provide summer shade for a circular seating area.

Although Goodhue's West Court, more often referred to as the West Millikan Mall, is one of the most visible entrances to the campus, it had long been neglected. In 1981, an anonymous donor offered to fund a new design. In place of concrete and ice plant, California live oaks and purple jacaranda trees alternate with beds of red roses and discreet parking areas for visiting Trustees. The sentinel-like cypress trees, which had become old and tired, were replaced with delicate wisteria plants trained to climb the arcade walls. The anonymous donor is now acknowledged in the area's new designation, the Bechtel Mall.

At the same time landscaping was used to bind together an eclectic mix of functional buildings in the modern campus. In the Goodhue campus the buildings form the edges of the main axis, but the San Pasqual pathway of the modern campus has uneven edges with buildings orientated in different directions. Using the concept of a green

forest to envelop the buildings, Land Images designed a free form pathway bordered by seating areas, grassy banks, colorful plantings, lily ponds and a variety of trees. To unite the engineering buildings of Watson, Steele and Keck, they created a mall with a serpentine path, grassy knolls and tall, elegant coast redwoods which mirror the vertical lines of the architecture.

For many years the Institute's geologists were disturbed by the fact that the rocks in and around the Throop garden pools were concrete imitations. In 1985, Caltech Associate Mrs. Dan Throop Smith, the great-granddaughter of Amos Throop, funded improvements to the Throop site. The money was used for reseeding the grass, putting in new plants and shrubs, refilling and stocking the pools with goldfish, and acquiring authentic rocks. Geologist Leon Silver (the W. M. Keck Foundation Professor for Resource Geology) organized a rock search. He selected specimens flushed out of the San Gabriel mountains into the Devil's Gate Dam near JPL.

The campus' open spaces and its landscaping are an important part of the 1989 Master Plan. The report includes an inventory of specimen trees within the campus boundaries and a recommended palette for trees, shrubs, vines, ground cover and turf. At the urging of Caltech's original leaders, Goodhue strove to integrate landscape and architecture. In the same spirit landscaping around new buildings should help to unify the open spaces between the buildings and be compatible with the rest of the campus.

Stephen Bechtel conceived a landscaping program which successfully pulled together the mixed architecture of the modern campus, and integrated the old with the new. Through his hard work and generosity Caltech now has the "atmosphere of scholarly calm and classic shade ever associated with the academic life" which Goodhue had envisioned. National and local honors have been awarded to Caltech for its campus beautification.

SCULPTURE

Caltech's first building, Throop Hall, set a precedent for incorporating sculpture on its facade. At the time of their installation the Calder Arches were considered one of the most important sculptural projects in Los Angeles. Goodhue's Spanish Renaissance theme included the use of cast-stone decoration over doorways and important windows. Kaufmann lavished his student dormitories with humorous figures and bas-relief sculpture. But, except for the occasional gift, the Institute has not collected free-standing sculpture.

Portrait sculptures of some of Caltech's leaders and important donors are scattered around the campus. In 1942 Holger Jensen and Helen Webster Jensen were paid $3,000 to create busts of Allan and Janet Balch. They look onto the Athenaeum's west patio from alcoves designed for them by Gordon Kaufmann. Two busts were made of Millikan. Mrs. Millikan felt that the one made by Joseph Portanova made "Dr. Millikan look troubled, elderly, insipid...not very happy and he looks like an old gentleman." This one now resides in the Archives. Allan and Janet Balch were so pleased with portraits the Jensens did of them that they immediately commissioned them to do a bust of Millikan. Mrs. Millikan liked this one

Throop Garden, 1985. The 40 authentic boulders at the Throop site are identified on a plaque. But Professor Silver says "there are some mysterious rocks that I don't understand. These will be a challenge for our geology students, and ultimately, some of them will solve the mystery." Every first year geology class makes a field trip through the gardens to find "books in the running brooks, sermons in stones, and good in everything."

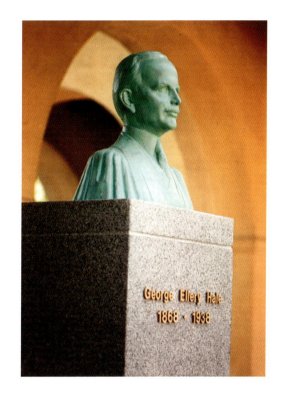

Sculpture of George Ellery Hale in the arcades between Dabney Hall and Parsons-Gates. Hale's bust is looking towards Mount Wilson and the Observatory which brought the great astronomer to Pasadena.

Sculpture of Robert Andrews Millikan in the arcades adjacent to the physics complex. When the Millikan Library was completed, the bust watched over meetings in the Board Room, until 1970 when it was moved to the location suggested by Mrs. Millikan.

and requested it be placed in the arcade near the Bridge Laboratory of Physics after her husband's death.

In 1987, a bust of George Ellery Hale, cast from the same mold as the Palomar Observatory statue, was donated to Caltech by members and friends of the Hale family and the Scherer-Hale Memorial Fund. Hale's daughter, Margaret, married Paul A. Scherer, the son of the first president of Throop Polytechnic Institute. Margaret gave Palomar the original bust, which was sculpted by Marian Brackenridge. Following the completion of the Beckman Institute in 1989, busts of Arnold and Mabel Beckman were sculpted by Peter Fagan of Urbana, Illinois. They were installed in a tiled alcove in the main entry lobby.

Tenjin, a bronze sculpture of a figure sitting on a water buffalo, used to stand in a small pond in front of the north wall of Dabney Garden. When the San Pasqual walkway was landscaped in 1981, the sculpture was moved to a shady corner inside Dabney Garden. Tenjin's history is complicated. In 1967, Edwin H. Schneider, a Los Angeles surgeon, died and left his estate, which included the Tenjin sculpture, to the Biology Division at Caltech. Dr. Schneider, an auction afficionado, had purchased the sculpture in 1951 from the estate of Adolph Bernheimer. Bernheimer, a member of the cotton milling family, made frequent trips to the Orient to acquire art. He paid $25,000 for the bronze statue of Tenjin in 1901. His collection was displayed in Oriental gardens at his estate in Pacific Palisades and became a famous tourist attraction. Bernheimer died in 1944, and his collection was auctioned in 1951 after the gardens had been abandoned because of cliff erosion.

For many years Caltech referred to its acquisition as "the Chinese philosopher Tenjin." However, after careful research it was discovered that the man on the water buffalo was not the philosopher Tenjin, nor was he Chinese. The figure represents Sugawara Michizane who was born in 845 A.D. in Japan. Michizane was a highly skilled poet and statesman whose career was ruined by the slander of a jealous political rival. To appease his vengeful spirit, which the people thought had caused a series of terrible calamaties, Michizane was posthumously deified and renamed Tenjin, meaning heavenly god. Eighty-four years later a shrine was erected to him in Kyoto.

Three small sculptures have discreet homes amongst the landscaping. "Lunar" by Aldo Casanova is centered below one of the lily ponds near Ramo Auditorium. It was given in 1974 by alumni George Tooby and David Steinmetz, and faculty member David Smith, who were members of a Baxter Art Gallery committee working on a sculpture program for the campus. A contribution was also made by the Pasadena and Foothill Chapter of the Women's Architectural League. The founding of the California Beta chapter of the Tau Beta Pi National Engineering Honor Society on June 11, 1921, at Caltech is marked by "The Bent," the society's symbol. This piece was placed on a grassy slope in the mall between Keck and Steele Engineering laboratories in 1988 or 1989. "Dynasty," an abstract bronze by Sorel Etrog, sits in a bed of colorful flowers along the San Pasqual walkway. It was presented in 1990 in memory of Harvey Eagleson, professor of English, by his friends and students.

For Caltech's centennial in 1991, a new sculpture was commissioned to replace a boat-shaped concrete fountain in the Millikan Pond. Individual trustees, alumni, associates, faculty and other friends of the Institute provided the funds for a stainless-steel kinetic sculpture named "Water Forms." The artist was Altadena resident

Statue of Tenjin on a water buffalo. Tenjin was really Sugawara Michizane born in AD. 845, the year of the buffalo. After his career as a poet and statesman had been ruined by a jealous rival, fires, floods and earthquakes plagued the country. To appease his spirit the people deified him as Tenjin. He is regarded as the deity of Japanese arts, sciences and learning, making him a suitable god for a garden at Caltech.

George Baker, who had been a professor of sculpture at Occidental College for 26 years and whose work has been exhibited worldwide.

One of the 1997 amendments to the current Master Plan stipulates that "Each time an Academic, Administrative or Athletic building over 70,000 square feet of gross floor area is constructed, Caltech shall include in the project a public art component equal to or greater than one percent of the construction cost." Alternatively, Caltech can contribute the money to an art fund administered by the Arts Commission.

Moore's Stone Volute was the Institute's first piece of public art. Installed between Noyes Laboratory and Beckman Behavioral Biology Laboratory, the piece is a part of Gordon Moore's engineering laboratory gift. Lloyd Hamrol, one of the foremost public artists in California, made the spiral shape, which is fifty feet in diameter, out of individual volcanic rocks called andesite collected near Ketchum, Idaho.

With an expansion program that includes several large buildings, Pasadena's new ordinance will bring an exciting collection of outdoor sculpture to the Institute.

Moore's *Stone Volute*, 1997. According to artist Lloyd Hamrol, the "earthwork will establish a territory of changing relationships meant to be physically explored." Children visiting the campus frequently enjoy walking along the top surface or running inside the curve of the spiral. A viewer standing in the center may feel embraced by the sculpture and experience a different outlook on the surrounding campus and its buildings.

Water Forms by George Baker. The piece is made up of six moving parts, each one mounted on ball bearings. The different sections are set in motion by wind, or through water pumped into a chamber below. The stainless steel shapes rock, tilt and turn. They reflect the light as arcs of water spout into the air. "My sculpture forms are subconsciously abstracted from the environment. Their movement is gentle. Their interaction is meant to produce a secluded, peaceful environment, and to elicit a contemplative mood," explains Baker.

CHAPTER TWENTY SEVEN

The Future

"ADVANCES IN THE BIOLOGICAL SCIENCES WILL HAVE THE SINGLE GREATEST IMPACT ON HUMAN EXPERIENCE IN THE COMING CENTURY. I WANT SOUTHERN CALIFORNIA TO BE A LEADER IN THIS CRITICALLY IMPORTANT FIELD, AND CALTECH IS UNIQUELY QUALIFIED TO SPEARHEAD THIS REMARKABLE NEW INITIATIVE."

— *Eli Broad*

With due pomp and ceremony, biologist David Baltimore was inaugurated as Caltech's sixth president on March 9, 1998. Baltimore was born in New York in 1938. He earned his undergraduate degree at Swarthmore College and his Ph.D. at Rockefeller University. In 1975, at the age of 37 he won the Nobel Prize in Physiology or Medicine for his research work on the genetics of viruses. Before coming to Caltech, Baltimore spent 25 years at MIT where he was the founding director of the Whitehead Institute for Biomedical Research.

At Caltech, Baltimore will balance running the Institute, managing a research laboratory and continuing as chairman of the AIDS vaccine research program for the National Institute of Health. Baltimore says that his "deepest goal as president is to maintain the essence of Caltech while helping it adapt to a changing world."

One of Baltimore's tasks during his first year in office was to establish a new fund-raising campaign. "Beyond the Genome, the Biological Sciences Initiative" was launched

with $5 million each from Camilla Chandler Frost and Benjamin M. Rosen, the campaign's trustee co-chairs. The campaign's goal is to raise $100 million for a new biological sciences building, new faculty positions in biological sciences and related disciplines, and to develop joint training programs with medical schools. Baltimore explained that "The 21st century will be the Golden Age of biology. We will see advances in both fundamental understanding of nature and medical technology for the treatment of disease."

By September of 1998 trustee Eli Broad donated half of the $36 million needed for the biological sciences center, the cornerstone of the program. Eli Broad is one of Southern California's most prominent civic and business leaders. He has been a Caltech trustee since 1993. His first business, Kaufman and Broad, a home-building company, made him a millionaire before he was 30 years old. Currently he is chairman and chief executive officer of SunAmerica Inc., a retirement savings powerhouse. He is also co-owner and co-chairman of the Sacramento Kings and ARCO Arena. Broad

David Baltimore became Caltech's sixth president on March 9, 1998 and will continue to run a research program. "I will be, I believe, the only functioning scientist who is running a major university in the United States."

has used his wealth to support education and the arts.

Caltech's new building will be called the Broad Center for the Biological Sciences. It will replace the Beckman Institute parking lot and will border the North Mall. The 100,000 square foot building will house about 10 research groups with offices, laboratories, lecture hall, seminar room, compact libraries and conference rooms. The high tech facilities will include an Imaging Center and a Biomolecular Structures Laboratory.

As a connoisseur of art and architecture, Broad is taking an active role in the design of the building. At his suggestion several prominent architects were asked to participate in a competition. Broad said, "The idea is to get a great piece of architecture that meshes aesthetically with the existing campus."

The firm of Pei Cobb Freed & Partners with James Freed as the principal designer was awarded the contract. They will work with SMP-SHG (Stone Marracinni Patterson and Smith Hinchman and Grylls) a San Francisco firm with an office in Santa Monica, as Executive Architects. Their brochure states, "Since the early 1950s, Pei Cobb Freed & Partners (formerly I. M. Pei & Partners) has completed over 150 major projects in more than 75 cities across the United States and around the world." Their projects include the East Building of the National Gallery of Art and the United States Holocaust Memorial Museum in Washington, D.C., the expansion of the Louvre Museum in Paris, and the Bank of China Tower in Hong Kong.

Although the firm is known for designing buildings with sharply angled planes and reflective glass, it also believes strongly in creating designs that meet the needs of a specific program, with buildings to fit their natural setting. For the Broad Center, James Freed is proposing a design that creates a transition between the past and the future. Traditional elements, which reflect Caltech's architectural heritage, will be blended with contemporary forms and materials.

Rendering of the Broad
Center for the Biological
Sciences. Proposed exterior
materials are stone, glass,
and etched stainless steel.

Amos Throop could never have envisioned that his humble "institution of public utility" based on his motto "Learn by Doing" would grow into the world famous California Institute of Technology. New challenges lie ahead as the Institute moves into the next millenium. Can this small, elite university maintain its place in the competitive world of research and funding without significant changes to its composition?

From the beginning, George Ellery Hale believed that architecture should be given a leading role in defining the school's ambition. The buildings and setting were to represent science as a humane endeavor, to inspire faculty and students to the highest standards, and to take advantage of the California climate. In the fulfillment of Hale's dream, Bertram Goodhue created the plan, theme, and academic core; and Gordon Kaufmann designed Caltech's social center and first residential complex. After an interlude of eclectism a new Master Plan has reintroduced the spirit of the original campus with its shaded portales, planted patios, sheltering walls, Spanish tile and Persian pools.

Beckman Institute's reflecting pool recalls the spirit of the original campus. The pool's blue tiles and delicately arched fountains remind us of Goodhue's wish for the West Court, "Were funds to permit, it would be most desirable to line this pool with blue glazed tile as commonly done in Persia and India."

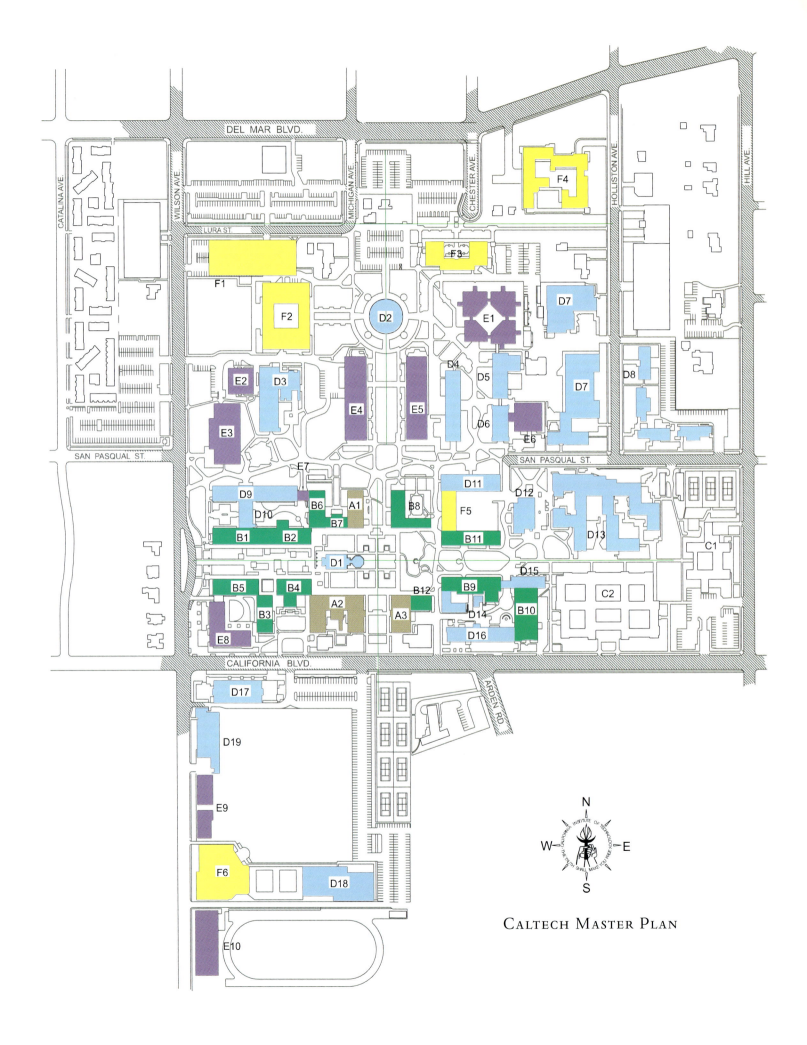

CALTECH MASTER PLAN

LEGEND

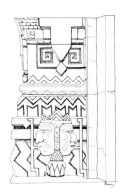

Bertram Goodhue 1917 - 1925

A1 Parsons-Gates Hall of Administration (Gates Chemistry)
A2 Bridge Laboratory (Physics)
A3 Sloan Laboratory (Mathematics & Physics)
    (High Voltage Research Laboratory)

Goodhue Associates 1925 - 1945

B1 Kerckhoff I (Biological Sciences)
B2 Kerckhoff II (Biological Sciences)
B3 Robinson Laboratory (Astrophysics & Astronomy)
B4 Arms Laboratory (Geological & Planetary Sciences)
B5 Mudd Laboratory - North (Geological & Planetary Sciences)
B6 Crellin Laboratory (Chemistry)
B7 Gates Annex (Chemistry)
B8 Dabney Hall (Development & Humanities)
B9 Guggenheim Laboratory (Aeronautics & Applied Physics)
B10 Synchrotron
B11 Thomas Laboratory (Civil & Mechanical Engineering)
B12 Kellogg Radiation Laboratory

Gordon Kaufmann 1929 - 1931

C1 Athenaeum
C2 South Student Houses

Modern Campus 1950's & 1960's

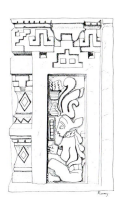

D1 Millikan Library
D2 Beckman Auditorium
D3 Noyes Laboratory (Chemical Physics)
D4 Keck Laboratories (Environmental Engineering & Materials Science)
D5 Steele Laboratory (Applied Physics & Electrical Engineering)
D6 Powell/Booth Computing Center
D7 Physical Plant
D8 Graduate Housing
D9 Church Laboratory (Chemical Biology)
D10 Alles Laboratory (Molecular Biology)
D11 Spalding Laboratory (Chemical Engineering)
D12 Winnett Student Center
D13 Undergraduate Dormitories
D14 Karman Laboratory (Fluid Mechanics & Jet Propulsion)
D15 Firestone Laboratory (Applied Mathmatics & Flight Sciences)
D16 Downs Lauritsen Laboratories (Physics & High Energy Physics)
D17 Keith Spalding Business Services
D18 Athletic Facilities
D19 Central Plant

Modern Campus 1970's & 1980's

E1 Watson Laboratories (Applied Physics)
E2 Mead Laboratory (Undergraduate Chemistry)
E3 Braun Laboratory (Cell Biology & Chemistry)
E4 Beckman Behavioral Biology
E5 Baxter Hall (Humanities & Social Sciences)
E6 Jorgensen Laboratory (Computer Science)
E7 Beckman Laboratory of Chemical Synthesis
E8 Mudd Laboratory - South (Geophysical & Planetary Sciences)
E9 Cooling Towers & Cogeneration
E10 David W. Morrisroe Astroscience Laboratory

New Master Plan 1989 -

F1 Broad Center (Biological Sciences)
F2 Beckman Institute
F3 Moore Laboratory (Engineering & Applied Science)
F4 Avery House
F5 Fairchild Library
F6 Braun Center (Gymnasium)

The Athenaeum ceilings were restored as this book was being prepared for press. In the main dining room, the removal of acoustical tiles, which had been installed in the ceiling's coffers during the 1960s, uncovered a blue-colored sponged tempera paint framed by an egg and dart design.

In the Hall of the Associates, the rosettes and ribs of the coffers were reguilded, the backdrop for the seals recolored, and a medallion-decorated frieze repainted. The restoration team consisted of Romy Wyllie, Interior Designer; Tony Heinsbergen, consultant; David Hunt and David Bell, artists.

BUILDING CHRONOLOGY

EARLY CAMPUS 1910-1945

YEAR	BUILDING	ARCHITECT	DONOR
1910	Throop Hall	Myron Hunt & Elmer Grey	Mr. Arthur Fleming Citizens of Pasadena
1971	Earthquake damage		
1973	Demolished		
1917	Gates Laboratory of Chemistry	Elmer Grey Bertram Grosvenor Goodhue	Messrs. C.W. Gates & P.G. Gates
1971	Earthquake damage		
1921	Culbertson Hall	Bertram Grosvenor Goodhue	Miss Kate Fowler Mrs. Marjorie Fleming Lloyd-Smith Pasadena Music & Art Association
1972	Demolished		
1922	Norman Bridge Laboratory of Physics 1st Unit (East Bridge)	Bertram Grosvenor Goodhue	Dr. Norman Bridge
1924	2nd Unit (Bridge Annex)		
1925	3rd Unit (West Bridge)		
1923	High Voltage Research Laboratory	Bertram Grosvenor Goodhue	Southern California Edison Company
1959	Retired		
1927	Gates Laboratory of Chemistry 2nd Unit (Gates Annex)	Mayers, Murray & Phillip (B.G.G. Associates) Clarence S. Stein	Messrs. C.W. Gates & P.G. Gates
1928	William G. Kerckhoff Laboratories of the Biological Sciences 1st Unit (West Kerckhoff)	Mayers, Murray & Phillip (B.G.G. Associates) Clarence S. Stein	Mr. William G. Kerckhoff Mr. Allan C. Balch General Education Board
1939	2nd Unit (East Kerckhoff)	Mayers, Murray & Phillip (B.G.G. Associates)	Miscellaneous donors
1928	Guggenheim Aeronautical Laboratory	Mayers, Murray & Phillip (B.G.G. Associates) Clarence S. Stein	Daniel Guggenheim Fund
1947	East Addition		
1928	Dabney Hall of the Humanities	Mayers, Murray & Phillip (B.G.G. Associates) Clarence S. Stein	Mr. & Mrs. Joseph B. Dabney
1930	Athenaeum	Gordon B. Kaufmann	Mr. & Mrs. Allan C. Balch
1931	Undergraduate Houses Blacker House Dabney House Fleming House Ricketts House	Gordon B. Kaufmann	Mr. & Mrs. R.R. Blacker Mr. & Mrs. Joseph B. Dabney 20 donors Dr. & Mrs. Louis D. Ricketts
1932	W.K. Kellogg Radiation Laboratory	Physical Plant Department Russell Porter	Mr. W.K. Kellogg
1932	Henry M. Robinson Laboratory of Astrophysics	Mayers, Murray & Phillip (B.G.G.Associates)	International Education Board (Rockefeller Foundation) General Education Board
1933	Optical Shop	Gustave W. Iser	IEB of the Rockefeller Foundation
1969	Synchrotron		

YEAR	BUILDING	ARCHITECT	DONOR
1933 1969	Machine Shop Demolished	Gustave W. Iser	IEB of the Rockefeller Foundation
1937	Crellin Laboratory of Chemistry	Mayers, Murray & Phillip (B.G.G. Associates)	Mr.& Mrs.E.W.Crellin
1938	Charles Arms Laboratory of the Geological Sciences	Mayers, Murray & Phillip (B.G.G. Associates)	Mr.& Mrs.Henry M. Robinson
1938	Seeley W. Mudd Laboratory of the Geological Sciences	Mayers, Murray & Phillip (B.G.G. Associates)	Mrs.Seeley W. Mudd

MODERN CAMPUS 1945-2000

YEAR	BUILDING	ARCHITECT	DONOR
1945 1950	Franklin Thomas Laboratory of Engineering 1st Unit 2nd Unit	Physical Plant Department	Eudora Hull Spaulding Trust (1st Unit) Institute Funds
1948	William G. Kerckhoff Laboratories of the Biological Sciences Annex	Physical Plant Department	Kerckhoff Laboratories Funds
1949 1973	Earhart Plant Research Laboratory [demolished]	Palmer Sabin	Earhart Foundation
1954	Alumni Swimming Pool	Marsh, Smith & Powell	Alumni Fund
1954	Scott Brown Gymnasium	Marsh, Smith & Powell	Scott Brown Trust
1955	Norman W. Church Laboratory for Chemical Biology	Stiles O. Clements	Norman W. Church Mrs. H. Robinson Mr. & Mrs.W. Kerckhoff
1957	Eudora Hull Spalding Laboratory of Engineering	Pereira & Luckman	Eudora Hull Spalding Trust
1957	Archibald Young Health Center	Physical Plant Department	Mrs. Archibald Young
1959	Physical Plant Building & Shops	Physical Plant Department	Many donors
1960	Gordon A. Alles Laboratory for Molecular Biology	Physical Plant Department	Dr. Gordon A. Alles Health Research Facilities Branch of National Institutes of Health
1960 1996	Campbell Plant Research Laboratory [demolished]	George Vernon Russell	Campbell Soup Company U.S. Public Health Service
1960	Undergraduate Houses: Lloyd House Page House Ruddock House	Charles Luckman & Associates Smith, Powell & Morgridge	Mr. & Mrs Ralph B. Lloyd Mr. James R. Page Mr. Albert B. Ruddock
1960	Harry Chandler Dining Hall	Charles Luckman & Associates Smith, Powell & Morgridge	Chandler family Pfaffinger Foundation Times Mirror Company
1960	Karman Laboratory of Fluid Mechanics & Jet Propulsion	Physical Plant Department Pereira & Associates	Aerojet-General Corporation.

YEAR	BUILDING	ARCHITECT	DONOR
1960	Alfred P. Sloan Laboratory of Mathematics & Physics (prev. High Volts)	Holmes & Narver	Alfred P. Sloan Foundation
1961	W. M. Keck Engineering Laboratories	Charles Luckman & Associates	W.M. Keck Foundation & Superior Oil Company of Los Angeles
1961	Graduate Houses Braun House Keck House Marks House Mosher-Jorgensen House	Smith, Powell & Morgridge	Carl F Braun Trust William M. Keck Jr David X. Marks Samuel B. Mosher & Earle M. Jorgensen
1962	Firestone Flight Sciences Laboratory	William L. Pereira & Associates	Firestone Tire & Rubber Company
1962 1998	Winnett Student Center Renovation	Smith, Powell & Morgridge A.C. Martin & Associates	Mr. P.G. Winnett Institute Funds
1963 1999	Willis H. Booth Computing Center Powell-Booth Laboratory for Computational Science	Neptune Thomas Associates Arthur Golding & Associates	Booth-Ferris Foundation National Science Foundation Charles Lee Powell Foundation
1964	Beckman Auditorium	Edward Durell Stone	Dr. & Mrs. Arnold O. Beckman
1966	Harry G. Steele Laboratory of Electrical Sciences	Langdon & Wilson	Harry G. Steele Foundation National Science Foundation
1966	Central Engineering Services Building	Davidson & Maurer	Institute Funds
1967	Robert A. Millikan Memorial Library	Flewelling & Moody	Dr. Seeley G. Mudd
1967	Arthur Amos Noyes Laboratory of Chemical Physics	Risley, Gould & Van Heuklyn	Mr. Chester F. Carlson National Science Foundation
1967	Central Plant	M.A. Nishkian & Co	Institute Funds
1969	George W. Downs Laboratory of Physics & Charles C. Lauritsen Laboratory of High Energy Physics	Neptune Thomas Associates	Mr. George W. Downs National Science Foundation Atomic Energy Commission
1969	Keith Spalding Building of Business Services	Wilton Becket & Associates	Institute Funds Named for Keith Spalding (Trustee)
1971	Donald E. Baxter, M.D. Hall of the Humanities & Social Sciences	Robert Alexander	Mrs. Delia B. Baxter U.S. Dept. Health, Education & Welfare Dr. & Mrs. Simon Ramo (Auditorium)
1971	The Earle M. Jorgensen Laboratory of Information Science	A. Quincy Jones Frederick E. Emmons	Mr. & Mrs. Earle M. Jorgensen Booth-Ferris Foundation + other donors.
1972 1981	Undergraduate Chemistry Laboratory Renovation - Clifford S. & Ruth A. Mead Memorial Undergraduate Chemistry Laboratory	John Kewell Associates O.K. Earl Corporation	Institute Funds Clifford S. & Ruth A. Mead Memorial Building Fund

YEAR	BUILDING	ARCHITECT	DONOR
1973	Central Plant - Cooling Towers & Cogeneration	Smith & Williams	Institute Funds
1974	The Mabel & Arnold Beckman Laboratories of Behavioral Biology	Robert C. Alexander	Dr. & Mrs. Arnold O. Beckman
1974	Seeley G. Mudd Building of Geophysics & Planetary Science (South Mudd)	George Vernon Russell & Associates.	Dr. Seeley G. Mudd Mrs. Roland Lindhurst Mr.& Mrs. Ross McCollum Mr.& Mrs. Henry Salvatori U.S. Deptartment of Health, Education & Welfare
1982	Thomas J. Watson, Sr., Laboratories of Applied Physics	Gyo Obata of Hellmuth, Obata & Kassabaum	Watson family + private donors
1982	Braun Laboratories in Memory of Carl F. & Winifred H. Braun	C F Braun & Co	Carl F Braun Trust + private donors National Cancer Institute
1983	Parsons-Gates Hall of Administration (Gates Laboratory of Chemistry rebuilt)	Bobrow/Thomas & Associates (BTA)	Ralph M. Parsons Foundation James Irvine Foundation
1984	Athletic Facility	O.K. Earl Corporation	Carl F Braun Trust Braun Foundation
1984,86, 88	Catalina Graduate Apartment Complex	O.K. Earl Corporation	Institute Funds + private donors
1986 1995	Infrared Processing & Analysis Center David W. Morrisroe Astroscience Laboratory Addition 2nd floor	Martin J. Jaska, Inc.	Institute Funds Dr. Arnold O.Beckman
1986	Beckman Laboratory of Chemical Synthesis	Physical Plant Department	Dr. & Mrs. Arnold O. Beckman
1989	Beckman Institute	Albert C. Martin & Associates	Dr. & Mrs. Arnold O. Beckman
1992	Braun Athletic Center	O.K. Earl Corporation	Braun Family Trust
1993	Parking Structure/ Satellite Utility Plant	Neptune Thomas Davis	Institute Funds
1996	The Gordon & Betty Moore Laboratory of Engineering	Neptune Thomas Davis	Dr. & Mrs. Gordon Moore
1996	Avery House	Moore Ruble Yudell	Mr. R. Stanton Avery
1997	Sherman Fairchild Library of Engineering & Applied Science	Moore Ruble Yudell	The Sherman Fairchild Foundation
1998	Winnett Student Center Rehab	AC Martin Partners	Institute Funds
2002	The Broad Center for the Biological Sciences	Pei Cobb Freed & Partners (Design Architects) SMP-SHG (Executive Architects)	Mr. Eli Broad + private donors

ACKNOWLEDGMENTS

It has been a privilege to write this book and I am deeply grateful to Thomas Everhart for conceiving the idea and asking me to tackle the project. As with all such undertakings there have been many contributors to whom I owe sincere thanks.

The Caltech Architectural Tour Service (CATS) grew out of a conference of Southland Campus Women's Clubs, which Caltech hosted in 1985, and for which I volunteered to design an architectural tour. Following this experiment Missy Jennings and I, together with the late Paula Samazan, decided to form an architectural tour service as a special offering of the Caltech Women's Club.

Initially we based our information on *Caltech 1910-1950: An Urban Architecture for Southern California.* This catalog was published in 1983 by the Institute's Baxter Art Gallery as part of an exhibit on Caltech's architecture organized by Jay Belloli, Stephanos Polyzoides and Peter de Bretteville. In addition, the original members of CATS did further research on the early campus architecture using material in local libraries, the Institute Archives and Physical Plant. Reports included interviews with faculty and visual surveys of buildings. Much of the archival information had been collected from many separate files of correspondence and organized into valuable architectural sourcebooks by Alice Stone. I am indebted to research done by Roxanna Anson, Jane Apostol, Jane Caughey, Bunny Gould, Missy Jennings, Linda Kamb, Theo Page, MaryJane Penzo, Paula Samazan, and Micheline Vogt. All CATS members, past and present, have contributed through their participation and dedication.

I am grateful for the encouragement and support of Robert O'Rourke and Paula DiConti of Public Relations and Judith Goodstein and Shelley Erwin of

Archives. As well as searching through files in the Institute Archives, I gathered much of the modern campus information from the Minutes of the Board of Trustees, which Mary Webster and the President's office staff allowed me to read. My search for archival illustrations was assisted by Shelley Erwin and Bonnie Ludt, and for contemporary illustrations by Pat Orr. Campus photographer, Robert Paz, responded cheerfully to my difficult requests and bravely balanced on a cherry picker to take some hard-to-reach bas-reliefs and medallions. Douglas Hill added an exciting dimension to the book with specialized interior shots and unusual architectural details. Mrs. Hugh Goodhue (Fanny) shared family memories and provided the photographs of her famous father-in-law.

No written production can succeed without critical readers. Jane Apostol, Bunny Gould and Micheline Vogt critiqued each section as it was written; Judith Goodstein read the manuscript for historical accuracy and Paula DiConti for political correctness; Bill Irwin and Mike McCallan of Physical Plant reviewed the information on the modern campus. Mike McCallan also gave unstintingly of his time to answer an assortment of questions and provide information on architects. Elvin Nixon searched for old architectural drawings and executed the coded campus plan.

Ann Gray, Balcony Press publisher, provided valuable advice and assistance throughout the project. And finally, I want to thank my husband, Peter, for his patience, guidance, encouragement and critical reading.

Bibliography

Balmori, Diana, Diane Kostial McGuire, Eleanor M. McPeck. *Beatrix Farrand's American Landscapes*. SagaPress, Inc. Sagaponack, New York, 1985.

Baxter Art Gallery. *Caltech 1910-1950: An Urban Architecture for Southern California*. California Institute of Technology, Pasadena, California, 1983.

Caltech Architecture Sourcebooks compiled by Alice Stone, 2 vols. Unpublished material available in the Archives of the California Institute of Technology, Pasadena, California.

Encyclopædia Brittanica, 15th Edition. Encyclopædia Britannica, Inc. William Benton, Publisher, 1943-1973. Printed in U.S.A., 1974.

Erwin, Shelley and Carol H. Bugé, editors. *The Amos Gager Throop Collection: A Guide to the Papers in The Archives of The California Institute of Technology and The Chicago Historical Society*. Institute Archives, California Institute of Technology, Pasadena, California 1990.

Fletcher, Bannister, Sir. *A History of Architecture on the Comparative Method*. 17th Edition, revised by R. A. Cordingley. Charles Scribner's Sons, New York. Reprinted 1963.

Gebhard, David and Robert Winter. *Los Angeles: An Architectural Guide*. Gibbs Smith, Publisher, Layton, Utah, 1994.

Gleye, Paul. *The Architecture of Los Angeles*. In collaboration with The Los Angeles Conservancy, Julius Shulman, and Bruce Boehner. Rosebud Books, the Knapp Press, Los Angeles, California, 1981.

Goodstein, Judith R. *Millikan's School*. W. W. Norton & Company, New York. London, 1991.

Goodstein, Judith R. and Alice Stone. *Caltech's Throop Hall*. The Friends of Caltech Libraries, Pasadena, California, 1981.

Oliver, Richard. *Bertram Grosvenor Goodhue*. The Architectural History Foundation New York. The MIT Press, Cambridge, Massachusetts and London, England, 1983.

Scheid, Ann. *Pasadena: Crown of the Valley*. Windsor Publications, Inc. Northridge, California, 1986.

Scully, Vincent, Jr. *Modern Architecture*. George Braziller, New York, 1967.

Scripps College. *Johnson, Kaufmann, Coate: Partners in the California Style*. Capra Press, Santa Barbara, California, 1992.

Stone, Edward Durell. *Recent and Future Architecture*. Horizon Press, New York, 1967.

Whitaker, Charles Harris, editor. *Bertram Grosvenor Goodhue - Architect and Master of Many Arts*. American Institute of Architects' Press, 1925; reissued, New York: Da Capo Press, 1976, with new introduction by Paul Goldberger.

Willard, Berton C. *Russell W. Porter, Arctic Explorer, Artist, Telescope Maker*. Bond Wheelwright Co., Freeport, Maine, c1976.

Winter, Robert. *Myron Hunt At Occidental College*. Occidental College, Los Angeles, California, 1986.

Yoch, James J. *Landscaping the American Dream: the Gardens and Film Sets of Florence Yoch, 1890-1972*. Harry N. Abrams Inc./ Sagapress Inc., 1989.

ILLUSTRATION CREDITS

Front cover: Photography by Douglas Hill

End sheets: Annamarie Mitchell

Title pages: Courtesy of the Archives, California Institute of Technology: 1; Robert J. Paz: 2, 3

Courtesy of the Archives, California Institute of Technology:
1, 4, 22, 23 bottom, 24, 28, 32, 33, 34, 36, 40, 41, 43, 47, 50, 54, 55, 56-7, 77, 83, 88, 93, 96-97, 98, 100, 108, 109 top, 112 top, 113, 127, 128 bottom, 131 top, 140, 144 top, 146, 147, 148, 153, 154, 168 top, 175, 180, 182 top, 187, 188, 193, 202, 203, 204, 225 bottom, 235, 255 bottom

Courtesy Physical Plant, California Institute of Technology:
48, 59, 84 bottom, 86, 129, 160, 182 bottom, 211, 214, 266

Courtesy Public Relations, California Institute of Technology:
17, 19, 23 top, 27, 49, 80, 87, 94, 95, 99, 102, 119, 131 bottom, 138 top, 144 bottom, 158-159, 167, 171, 178 top, 179, 194, 199, 205, 207, 209, 236, 249, 256

Courtesy Development, California Institute of Technology:
183

Courtesy The Athenaeum, California Institute of Technology:
137

Karel Bauer, courtesy Caltech Archives:
196

Bennett-Kennedy Photographers, Pasadena, courtesy Caltech Archives:
132

Bachrach, courtesy Caltech Public Relations:
217

Clemens of Copenhagen, courtesy Caltech Public Relations:
201

Peggy Firth, courtesy Caltech Graphic Arts Facilities:
151

Portraiture by Carl A. Gist, courtesy Caltech Archives:
39, 42, 107, 138 bottom

Courtesy Mrs. Hugh Goodhue:
31, 62 top, 64

Courtesy Roy Gould:
210 top

Kurt Hauser:
10

Douglas Hill Photography:
6, 8, 12, 15, 29, 45, 65, 72, 76, 82, 85, 89, 90, 91, 103, 105, 114L, 125, 133, 134, 141, 149, 161, 164, 169, 172, 181, 215, 217, 220, 221, 239, 254, 264, 268, 274, 277

Hiller Studios, Pasadena, courtesy Caltech Archives:
26, 73, 74, 128 top

Peter A. Juley & Son Collection, National Museum of Art, Smithsonian Institution:
84 top, 115, 116, 178 bottom, 186

Land Images:
250, 251, 253

Gerald Landry:
81

O. S. Marshall, courtesy Caltech Archives:
101

W. Albert Martin, Pasadena, courtesy Caltech Archives:
117

Meyer & Allen Associates:
218, 238

Annamarie Mitchell:
71

Tony O'Keefe, Architectural Photographer:
226, 228

William Olson, courtesy Caltech Archives:
168 bottom

Robert J. Paz, courtesy Caltech Archives:
69

Robert J. Paz:
2, 63, 109 bottom, 110, 111, 112 bottom, 114R, 118, 120,
122, 124, 130, 155, 190, 206, 210 bottom, 212, 213, 225 top
L, 227, 231, 232, 233, 237, 243, 244, 245, 246, 247, 255 top,
258, 259, 261

Pei Cobb Freed & Partners, courtesy Caltech Physical
Plant:
263

R. V. Smutny, courtesy Caltech Archives:
62 bottom

Edward Durell Stone, courtesy Caltech Archives:
189

Romy Wyllie:
44, 46, 75, 104, 121, 123, 152, 165, 191, 198, 224, 225 top R,
229, 262, 265, 267, 287

NOTES

The following abbreviations are used:
AS, Alice Stone Sourcebooks, CIT Archives; CIT, California Institute of Technology;
GEH, George Ellery Hale Papers, CIT Archives;
LADuB, Lee Alvin DuBridge Papers, CIT Archives.
Abbreviated book citations in the notes are listed in full in the bibliography.

PART I — THE EARLY YEARS
CHAPTER 1. SMALL BEGINNINGS
Page 17   Headquote: Amos Throop's letter to cousin Cordelia in Iowa. 1892. Quoted by Martha Vaughan Smith in a speech at the Inauguration of President Baltimore, March 9, 1998. Historical Files, FF11.2, CIT Archives.

Page 17   ("To furnish students...") Quoted in Shelley Erwin and Carol H. Bugé, eds. *The Amos Gager Throop Collection: A Guide to the Papers in the Archives of The California Institute of Technology and the Chicago Historical Society.* P.13. 1990.

CHAPTER 2. NEW DIRECTIONS
Page 21   Headquote: James A. B. Scherer. "The Throop Idea" in *The Arroyo Craftsman*, Vol.1, No.1, October 1909. AS.

Page 23   ("The Throop Idea...") Ibid.

Page 21   ("He spends the major...") "Hand, Eye and Brain" in *Land of Sunshine*, January 1902. Ibid.

Page 22   ("concentrate their entire...") ("adequate instruction...") Quoted in Judith R. Goodstein *Millikan's School.* P.30. G. E. Hale to G. V. Wendell, Jan 13, 1908.

Page 23   ("a high-grade institute...") Quoted in Judith R. Goodstein *Millikan's School.* P.33. Hale to Scherer, May 9, 1908.

Page 23   ("a business man's...") Robert Winter *Myron Hunt at Occidental College* P.12. 1986.

Page 24   ("Mr. Grey took up...") Ibid.

Page 25   ("We are mentally...") Quoted in Alice Stone and Judith R. Goodstein "Windows Back of a Dream" p.7. *CIT 1910-1950: An Urban Architecture for Southern California.* Baxter Art Gallery, 1983.

Page 25   ("An expensive luxury...") Myron Hunt to James A. B. Scherer, August 10, 1908. AS.

Page 24   ("A dome was necessary...") The Independent, New York, February 6, 1913. Historical Files 34.2, CIT Archives.

Page 26   ("Beginning with the spandrel...") Alexander Stirling Calder, Sculptor "Description of the Sculptural Archways." AS.

Page 28   ("the building which...") Quoted in Judith R. Goodstein and Alice Stone. The Friends of CIT Libraries *CIT's Throop Hall.* P. 47. 1981.

PART II — BERTRAM GOODHUE
CHAPTER 3 - GOODHUE'S MASTER PLAN
Page 31   Headquote: George Ellery Hale in *Bertram Grosvenor Goodhue - Architect and Master of Many Arts*, edited by Charles Harris Whitaker. American Institute of Architects, Inc. 1925.

Page 31   ("Seeing this, and ...") Ibid.

Page 31   ("aesthetic failure of...") Alson Clark "CIT and Southern California Architecture" P.43. *CIT 1910-1950: An Urban Architecture for Southern California.* Baxter Art Gallery, 1983.

Page 32   ("slight, blond, blue-eyed...") Bertram Grosvenor Goodhue in *Dictionary of American Biography, Vol.VII*, edited by Allen Johnson and Dumas Malone. Published under the Auspices of American Council of Learned Societies. Charles Scribner's Sons, New York, 1931.

Page 35   ("elastic...") Scherer to Goodhue, October 12, 1915. AS.

Page 35   ("virtually govern the layout...") Scherer to Goodhue, October 5, 1915. AS.

Page 35   ("What I mean is...") Hale to Goodhue, March 2, 1916. AS.

Page 35   ("or, as the Spanish...") Goodhue, *A Report to Accompany the General Block Plan.* No date. AS.

Page 35   ("We have not hesitated...") Ibid.

Page 37   ("false, in that it...") Ibid.

Page 37   ("through the great central") Ibid.

Page 37   ("this fixed condition") Scherer to Goodhue, November 24, 1915. AS.

Page 37   ("We might end up...") Scherer to Fleming, December 10, 1915. AS.

Page 37   ("The central long court...") Goodhue to Scherer, December 9, 1916. AS.

CHAPTER 4. CHEMISTRY AND PHYSICS

Page 39   Chemistry Headquote: Board of Trustees Resolution. CIT, 1936.

Page 40   ("frontispiece, fenestration and...") Goodhue to Scherer, January 24, 1916. AS.

Page 40   ("his pet modeller ...") Goodhue to Scherer, April 27, 1916. AS.

Page 42   Physics Headquote: E. C. Watson, *Science Progress* (England), October, 1925. AS.

Page 46   ("It will be available...") CIT Bulletin, December 1923. CIT Archives.

Page 51   ("The first laboratory...") *Engineering and Science*, February 1949, CIT.

Page 51   ("There must be...") Millikan to Goodhue, February 10, 1922. AS

CHAPTER 5. CULBERTSON HALL

Page 53   Headquote: President Scherer's Annual Report, 1911-1912. AS.

CHAPTER 6. AN UNTIMELY DEATH

Page 61   Headquote. Hale in a telegram to Mrs. Bertram G. Goodhue, April 24, 1924. AS.

Page 61   ("the financial condition...") Minutes of the Executive Council, December 19, 1931. AS.

Page 61   ("Lawrie's sketch is...") Millikan to Hardie Phillip, December 19, 1931. AS.

Page 63   ("to provide the atmosphere...") Goodhue, *A Report to Accompany the General Block Plan*. No date. AS.

Page 64   ("Goodhue was generally...") Hale to Harry Chandler, June 23, 1925. AS.

Page 64   ("The possibilities of...") Hale in *Bertram Grosvenor Goodhue - Architect and Master of Many Arts* edited by Charles Harris Whitaker. American Institute of Architects, Inc. 1925.

PART III — GOODHUE ASSOCIATES

CHAPTER 7. A NEW RELATIONSHIP

Page 67   Headquote: Gano Dunn to Robert Millikan, August 14, 1924. AS.

Page 68   ("Evidently it is a case...") Ibid.

Page 67   ("Hale and Noyes promised...") Judith R. Goodstein in *Millikan's School*. P.94.

Page 68   ("We have got a tradition...") Francis Mayers to Gano Dunn, August 22, 1924. AS.

Page 68   ("Our distance from New York...") Hale to Fleming, October 28, 1927. AS.

Page 68   ("It should be perfectly...") Ibid.

Page 68   ("I do mean that the style ...") Ibid.

CHAPTER 8. CHEMISTRY ADDITIONS

Page 71   Headquote: Arthur Fleming to Hardie Phillip, July 10, 1925. AS.

Page 73   ("We have got a real...") Noyes to Hale, September 4, 1925. AS.

Page 73   ("je prends mon ...") Goodhue in *A Report to Accompany the General Block Plan*. No date. AS.

CHAPTER 9. AERONAUTICS

Page 79   Headquote: *Engineering and Science*, January 1966. CIT.

Page 80   ("the aircraft capital...") Judith R. Goodstein in *Millikan's School*. P.177.

CHAPTER 10. HUMANITIES

Page 83   Headquote: Noyes to Hale, June 8, 1926. AS.

Page 83   ("A Hall of the Humanities...") Ibid.

Page 86   ("for it must be...") Ibid.

Page 83   ("through a fundamental training...") Millikan to F. C. Austin. July 21, 1928. AS.

Page 84   (the office sciographer..caster of..") Bertram Goodhue quoted in "Twelfth-Night in Mr. Goodhue's Office" *Pencil Points*, Vol.III, No.2, February 1922.

Page 86   ("Classes in literature...") William B. Munro "Dabney Hall: Giving the Humanities Their Proper Place" in Bulletin of CIT, Vol.XXXVII, No. 118, January 1928. CIT Archives.

Page 90   ("Stein is much better...") Hale to Morgan, February 24, 1928. AS.

CHAPTER 11. ASTROPHYSICS

Page 93   Headquote: Hale to Morgan. August 12, 1929. AS.

Page 96   ("simplicity seems ...") Hale to Porter, March 14, 1930. AS.

Page 97   ("gem of the Institute group.") Porter to Hale, September 11, 1929. AS.

Page 104   ("an old astronomical...") Webster's New Collegiate Dictionary, 1980.

CHAPTER 12. BIOLOGY AND GEOLOGY

Page 107   Biology headquote: Hardie Phillip to Thomas Hunt Morgan September 12, 1927. AS.

Page 107   ("This domed building...") Hale to Fleming, October 28, 1927. AS.

Page 113   ("strict imitation...") Helen Searing "From Arcady to Anarchy: American College Architecture Between the Wars" *CIT 1910-1950: An Urban Architecture for Southern California*. Baxter Art Gallery, 1983.

Page 115   Geology headquote: California Institute of Technology Bulletin, 1925. Historical Files S3.1, CIT Archives.

Page 115   ("The region likewise...") Ibid.

Page 115   ("field work in...") Ibid.

Page 116   ("perfectly feasible..") Hardie Phillip quoted in the Minutes of the Board of Trustees, October 26, 1929. AS.

Page 116   ("recognized as one...") Mr. J. B. Lippincott, April 13, 1939. John & Imra Buwalda Papers, Box 2, CIT Archives.

Page 117   ("under circumstances existing...") Minutes of the Board of Trustees, December 2, 1931. AS.

Page 117   (erection of the Chemistry...") Ibid.

Page 118 ("When you generously...") John P.
   Buwalda to Harvey S. Mudd, June 19, 1939. John
   & Imra Buwalda Papers, Box 2, CIT Archives.

Page 121 ("After years of being...") Millikan at the
   dedication of the Seeley W. Mudd and The
   Charles Arms Laboratories of the Geological
   Sciences, March 14, 1939. Historical Files S3.1, CIT
   Archives.

PART IV — GORDON KAUFMANN
CHAPTER 13. THE ATHENAEUM

Page 127 Headquote: Athenaeum Handbook, 1931.
   Historical Files S1.6, CIT Archives.

Page 128 ("There is in Southern...") Undated and
   unauthored document. AS.

Page 128 ("to hear discussions...") Ibid.

Page 129 ("some blue prints of...") Goodhue to Hale,
   June 5, 1923. AS.

Page 129 ("the other corner...") Ibid.

Page 129 ("Designs have just...") Newspaper
   (unidentified) article. March 30, 1925. Historical
   Files S2.4, CIT Archives.

Page 131 ("should be done by...") Minutes of the
   Executive Council, Board of Trustees, February
   21, 1928. AS.

Page 131 ("I am convinced that...") Hale to Balch,
   March 7, 1928. AS.

Page 131 ("I assume, of course,...") Ibid.

Page 135 ("as designed by Mr. Goodhue...") Noyes
   quoted in the Minutes of the Board of Trustees,
   March 13, 1928. AS.

Page 136 ("Ariel of architecture") Thomas A.
   Talmadge quoted in Alson Clark "The
   'Californian' Architecture of Gordon B.
   Kaufmann." *Review*, Society of Architectural
   Historians, Southern California Chapter. Vol.1,
   No 3, Summer 1982. AS.

Page 136 ("these [Mediterranean] details with...") Jan
   Furey Muntz "Gordon B. Kaufmann: California
   Classicism" in *Johnson, Kaufmann, Coate: Partners
   in the California Style*. Scripps College, 1922.

Page 139 ("As the architecture...") Ibid.

Page 140 ("the Athenaeum acts like...") Ibid.

Page 136 ("The location on the central...") Gordon
   Kaufmann *Report On The Sketches For The Proposed
   Athenaeum For The California Institute of
   Technology*. Undated. AS.

Page 136 ("close the most important...") Ibid.

Page 136 ("For the purposes of...") Ibid.

Page 138 ("woven for the palace...") Undated note.
   Historical Files S1.7, CIT Archives.

Page 139 ("You will notice that...") Hale to Munro,
   July 2, 1930. Paul Epstein Papers 2.3, CIT Archives.

Page 139 ("We believe that the...") Theodore A.
   Heinrich, Robert O. Schad and James R. Page
   (Board of Experts Huntington Library staff) to
   the Trustees of the California Institute of
   Technology, February 5, 1951. Minutes of the
   Board of Trustees, CIT.

Page 139 ("it was not appropriate...") Minutes of the
   Athenaeum Board of Governors, February 18,
   1975. Athenaeum, CIT.

Page 140 ("Mr. Balch expressed his desire...")
   Minutes of the Executive Council, Board of
   Trustees, May 31, 1930. AS.

CHAPTER 14.
UNDERGRADUATE DORMITORIES

Page 143 Headquote: Grant V. Jenkins to Donald S.
   Clark, October 25, 1958. Historical Files S2.9, CIT
   Archives.

Page 143 ("under close oversight...") Annual Report
   1909-1910. Ibid.

THE SOUTH STUDENT HOUSES

Page 145 Headquote: Millikan to Harry Chandler,
   February 6, 1929. AS.

Page 145 ("In this way all...") Special Committee (to
   study the problem of undergraduate life at the
   Institute) to the Board of Trustees, March 21,
   1928. AS.

Page 146 ("the proper provision for...") Ibid.

Page 145 ("In these halls...") Millikan to Mr. F. C.
   Austin, July 21, 1928. AS.

Page 146 ("three other public...") Millikan to Harry
   Chandler, February 6, 1929. AS.

Page 146 ("growing out of Mr. Goodhue's...") Ibid.

Page 146 (The Institute..will ultimately...") Ibid.

Page 147 ("As you will see...") Goodhue to Hale,
   June 5, 1923. AS.

Page 150 ("Kaufmann did not try...") *Engineering and
   Science*, November/December 1979, CIT.

Page 150 ("Each court was an...") Joseph Giovannini
   "Gordon Kaufmann" *CIT 1910-1950: An Urban
   Architecture for Southern California*. Baxter Art
   Gallery, 1983.

CHAPTER 15.
LANDSCAPING THE EARLY CAMPUS

Page 157 Headquote: Beatrix Farrand to Arthur
   Fleming, March, 1928. AS.

Page 157 ("govern the layout...") Scherer to
   Goodhue, October 5, 1915. AS.

Page 160 ("to make the plan...") quoted in Balmori,
   McGuire, and McPeck *Beatrix Farrand's American
   Landscapes*, 1985.

Page 160 ("As I think over...") Farrand to Fleming,
   March, 1928. AS.

Page 160 ("seductive Spanish garden..") Pasadena
   Star News, September 27, 1928.

Page 162 ("I hope the Institute...") Farrand to
   Millikan, November 15, 1932. AS.

Page 162 ("so that a vista...") Campus Planting - Mrs.
   Farrand's recommendations listed in the Minutes
   of the Executive Council, Board of Trustees, July
   6, 1937. AS.

Page 162 ("The levels, etc. have been...") William
   Munro to Farrand, November 19, 1938. AS.

Page 162 ("I do not feel...") Farrand to Millikan, March 24, 1938. AS.

Page 162 ("As you have doubtless...") Farrand to Munro, July 19, 1938. AS.

Page 162 ("able, highly-trained...") Myron Hunt quoted by James J. Yoch in "Harmony and Invention in the Gardens of Florence Yoch" *Pacific Horticulture*, 1989.

Page 162 ("She designed gardens...") Ibid.

Page 163 ("An olive, a cypress...") Ibid.

Page 163 ("became an important...") Robert Smaus "California Essence" *Los Angeles Times* magazine, August 20, 1989.

PART V — THE MODERN CAMPUS
CHAPTER 16. CHANGING OF THE GUARD

Page 171 Headquote: Judith R. Goodstein *Millikan's School*. P.262.

Page 172 ("explaining science to the...") Ibid.

Page 172 ("The Institute..gave...") Lee DuBridge quoted by Betsy Woodford in *On Campus*, CIT. October 4, 1995.

THE PEREIRA LUCKMAN PLAN

Page 173 Headquote: Lee DuBridge quoted in *Engineering & Science*, December 1952.

Page 174 ("appeared to herald...") John Morris Dixon in *Progressive Architecture*, January 1988.

Page 174 ("the triumphant new architecture...") Ibid.

Page 174 ("Dr. Millikan has been...") Ann Bacon oral history. Historical Files S2.13, CIT Archives.

Page 174 ("I am now 12 years old..") Minutes of the Board of Trustees, CIT. February 23, 1958.

Page 175 ("Our country is now engaged...") Brochure "Unconquered Worlds" Historical Files K3.7, CIT Archives.

Page 175 ("High Volts could be...") Lee DuBridge. Quoted in Minutes of the Board of Trustees, CIT. May 6, 1957.

CHAPTER 17.
PLAIN & DECORATED BOXES

Page 177 Headquote: Lee DuBridge at the ground-breaking ceremony for Physical Plant, September 16, 1958. Historical Files S3.2, CIT Archives.

Page 177 ("a significant element...") Ibid.

Page 177 ("the actual ground-breaking...") Ibid.

Page 180 ("the round surfaces...") Minutes of the Board of Trustees, CIT. October 7, 1963.

CHAPTER 18. AN AUDITORIUM

Page 185 Headquote: Lee DuBrige to Dr. James R. Killian at MIT, March 2, 1964. LADuB 55.13.

Page 190 ("a thing of great...") Ibid.

Page 188 ("distinguished speakers, demonstra-tion...") Faculty Planning Panel to DuBridge, *Recommendations for Consideration by Architect in Design for Beckman Auditorium*, June 17, 1959. LADuB 56.2.

Page 188 ("Acoustice planning should ...") Ibid.

Page 188 ("an all-white circular...") Edward Durell Stone *Recent & Future Architecture*. 1967.

Page 188 ("It does seem to me strange...") Vern O. Knudsen to DuBridge, November 22, 1961. LADuB 56.2.

Page 190 ("From Spanish Tile...") Dedication speech by George Beadle. LADuB 55.13.

Page 190 ("The consensus was that...") Oscar Mandel, Charles Newton and J. Kent Clark in *Report on the Use of the Beckman Auditorium for Professional Theatrical Productions*, February 1964. LADuB 56.5.

Page 190 ("Musicians, dancers, and actors...") *East of Lake West of the Moon*. Brochure of the Performing Arts Series, 1998-99 Season. Office of Public Events, CIT.

CHAPTER 19. A CENTRAL LIBRARY

Page 193 Headquote: Dr. Seeley Mudd to Mr. Ruddock and Dr. DuBridge, March 24, 1959. Minutes of the Board of Trustees, CIT.

Page 195 ("It is understood that...") Ibid.

Page 195 ("All present from CIT...") Pereira and Luckman meeting memorandum, April 12, 1954. Institute Libraries 18.2, CIT Archives.

Page 194 ("DuBridge does not wish...") Ibid.

Page 195 ("library should be a...") DuBridge quoted in Minutes of the Board of Trustees, CIT. July 12, 1954.

Page 194 ("The exterior of the building...") Minutes of the Board of Trustees, CIT. May 25, 1959.

Page 195 ("the library contract...") Minutes of the Board of Trustees, CIT. February 2, 1959.

Page 195 ("The big news of the week...") Minutes of the Board of Trustees, CIT. April 6, 1959.

Page 197 ("The library building would...") Alan Blumenthal to DuBridge, February 10, 1965. LADuB 89.7.

Page 197 ("During all of these last...") DuBridge to Members of the Faculty, March 19, 1965. LADuB 89.13.

Page 198 ("He spent untold...") Arnold Beckman at the Dedication of the Library, June 9, 1967. LADuB 89.15.

CHAPTER 20. THE ALEXANDER PLAN

Page 201 Headquote: Robert E. Alexander, Master Plan Report, 1971 included in Minutes of the Board of Trustees, CIT. October 29-31, 1971.

Page 201 ("campus master plan...") Charles Luckman quoted in Minutes of the Board of Trustees, CIT. January 6, 1964.

Page 201 ("to work on long-range...") Buildings and Grounds Report, January 10, 1966. Minutes of the Board of Trustees, CIT.

Page 201 ("was one of the most...") Robert Alexander obituary, *Los Angeles Times*, December 2, 1992.

Page 202 ("The California Institute of Technology believes...") Court of Man in *Science for Mankind Development Program*, 1967-1968. Historical Files K3.9, CIT Archives.

Page 203 ("to bring the women..."). Report on Admission of Women, Minutes of the Board of Trustees, CIT. October 6, 1969.

Page 203 ("the recent earthquake...") Harold Brown quoted in Minutes of the Board of Trustees, CIT. February 9, 1971.

Page 203 ("If the ground shaking...") Memorandum of December 30, 1968 from George Housner and Paul Jennings to Royal Tyson quoted in Minutes of the Buildings and Grounds Committee, CIT. February 3, 1969.

CHAPTER 21. THE GOLDBERGER ERA

Page 209 Headquote: Minutes of the Board of Trustees, CIT. June 14, 1974.

Page 209 ("Work in theoretical...") Inauguration brochure, October 27, 1979. Historical Files FF1.1, CIT Archives.

Page 209 ("Among those who...") Ibid.

Page 211 ("the desire to recall...") Braun Corporation representative quoted in Minutes of the Buildings and Grounds Committee. Board of Trustees, CIT. December 4, 1978.

Page 212 ("Caltech has made an important..") Michael Bobrow quoted in *Around the Campus*, CIT. February 1983.

PART VI — A NEW MASTER PLAN
CHAPTER 22. THE 1989 MASTER PLAN

Page 217 Headquote: CIT Master Plan, July 1989. Physical Plant Department, CIT.

Page 217 ("nonprofit institutions occupying...") Ibid.

Page 217 ("the most comprehensive...") *On Campus*, CIT. September 1986.

Page 220 ("attitude..should be a...") CIT Master Plan, 1989.

CHAPTER 23. THE NORTH CAMPUS

Page 223 The Beckman Institute - Headquote: CIT Master Plan, 1989.

Page 226 The Moore Laboratory - Headquote: Dedication program, CIT. January 9, 1996.

Page 227 ("unique, state-of-the-art...") Ibid.

Page 228 ("Investigators in the...") Ibid.

Page 230 Avery House - Headquote: Invitation to the Groundbreaking Ceremony, CIT. May 9, 1995.

Page 233 ("provided the resources to...") *CIT News*. Volume 31, No 4, 1997.

CHAPTER 24. THE SOUTH CAMPUS

Page 235 Headquote: Millikan to the Board of Trustees, March 10, 1922. AS.

Page 235 ("the long-talked-of CIT...") *Pasadena Star News*, April 23, 1937. Historical Files S2.3, CIT Archives.

Page 236 ("the voters of Pasadena...") *Engineering and Science Monthly*, March 1947. p.12.

CHAPTER 25. INFILLS AND RENOVATIONS

Page 241 Headquote: CIT Master Plan, 1989.

Page 241 ("an astute businessman...") *On Campus*. CIT. Jan 1997, Vol. 13, No.5.

Page 247 ("to create the...") Winnett Student Center brochure. CIT. 1998.

CHAPTER 26. OPEN SPACES

Page 249 Headquote: Stephen Bechtel in report from the Buildings and Grounds Committee to Board of Trustees. Minutes of the Board of Trustees, CIT. October 27-29, 1978.

Page 249 ("indicated he hoped ...") Ibid

Page 252 ("atmosphere of scholarly...") Goodhue, *A Report to Accompany the General Block Plan*. No date. AS.

Page 255 ("there are some mysterious...") Leon Silver quoted in *CIT News*, February 1985.

Page 255 ("books in the running...") Shakespeare. *As You Like It*. II,i,12.

SCULPTURE

Page 255 ("Dr. Millikan looks troubled,..") Edythe Baker memorandum on telephone conversation with Mrs. Robert A. Millikan, Spring of 1953. LADuB 110.7.

Page 257 ("the Chinese philosopher Tenjin") Quoted in "Tenjin: a case of mistaken identity?" *On Campus*, CIT. 1990.

Page 259 ("My sculpture forms...") George Baker quoted in "Kinetic sculpture commissioned for centennial" *On Campus*, CIT. October 1990

Page 259 ("Each time an Academic...") CIT Amended Master Plan, 1997.

Page 259 ("earthwork will establish...") Lloyd Hamrol quoted in *On Campus*, CIT. October, 1997

CHAPTER 27. THE FUTURE

Page 261 Headquote: Eli Broad quoted in *News Release* by Office of Public Relations, CIT. September 15, 1998.

Page 261 ("deepest goal as president..") David Baltimore quoted by Heidi Aspaturian in "An Interview with David Baltimore", *On Campus*, CIT. April 1998.

Page 261 ("The 21st century will...") David Baltimore quoted in *On Campus*, CIT. June 1998.

Page 261 ("I will be, I believe...") David Baltimore quoted by Robert Lee Hotz in "Biomedicine's Bionic Man" *Los Angeles Times Magazine*, September 28, 1997.

Page 262 ("The idea is to get a great...") Eli Broad quoted in *CIT News*, Volume 32, No. 3, 1998.

Page 262 ("Since the early 1950s,...") "Introduction to the Firm" in Brochure of Pei Cobb Freed & Partners, September, 1998. Physical Plant Department, CIT.

Page 265 ("Were funds to permit...") Goodhue, *A Report to Accompany the General Block Plan*. No date. AS.

Index

aeronautical engineering 79, 177
Albert C. Martin & Associates 223, 246-247
Alexander, Robert E. 10, 201-203, 205-207, 209, 219
Alfred P. Sloan Foundation 179
Allen, Clifton 219
Alles Laboratory of Molecular Biology 177
Allison, John & David 131
alumni 13, 235-236, 239, 257
American Institute of Architects 64, 155
American-Indian 75
Andalusia 136, 246
Apollo 26, 28, 204-205, 237, 239
arcade 25, 40, 51, 111, 149, 180, 247, 252, 257
archives 128, 138, 197, 255
armillary sphere 100
Arms, Charles 116, 119, 121, 162, 202
Arroyo Seco 80, 116
art deco 62, 88
art museum 33, 53-54
Art Nouveau 174
Astrophysics Laboratory 9, 67, 76, 93-95, 97, 99-100, 102-104, 146, 166
Athena 127, 139
Athenaeum 9, 69, 127-129, 131-132, 135-141, 146, 150, 155, 162-163, 165-166, 187, 220, 224, 252, 255
athletic facilities 35, 173, 203, 219-220, 235-237, 239, 259
Atomic Energy Commission 181
auditorium 10, 21, 33, 53-55, 58, 107, 115-116, 177, 185-190, 202, 206-207, 209, 219-220, 223-224, 227, 257
Austin, F.C. 145
Avery Endowment Fund 230
Avery House 230-231, 233
Avery, Stanton R. 230-231, 233
Bacher, Robert 171-172, 174
Baker, George 259
Balboa Park 31
Balch Graduate School of the Geological Sciences 128
Balch, Allan and Janet 128
Baldeschwieler, John 211
Balmori, McGuire & McPeek 160
Baltimore, David 14, 261
baroque 40
Bateman House 203, 211
Baxter Art Gallery 257
Baxter Hall 88, 206

Baxter, Mrs. Donald 206
Beadle, George 172, 174, 190
Beaux Arts 25, 61
Bechtel Mall 251-252
Bechtel, Stephen D. 219, 249-252
Beckman Auditorium 188-190, 202, 206, 219-220, 223, 227
Beckman Institute 197, 223-227, 246, 257, 262, 265
Beckman Laboratories of Behavioral Biology 202, 206, 259
Beckman Laboratory of Chemical Synthesis 212-213
Beckman, Arnold and Mabel 174, 185, 190, 198, 206, 212-213, 257
Bernheimer, Adolph 257
Beyond the Genome 261
Big Bear 104
Biology 9, 67, 107-109, 111, 113-117, 119, 121, 128, 166, 172, 174-175, 177, 179, 202, 206, 211, 219, 223, 226, 239, 247, 257, 259, 261
Blacker House 150, 203
Blacker, Robert Roe 143, 146
Blumenthal, Alan 196-197
Board of Trustees 13, 22-23, 25, 39, 42, 53, 73, 108, 128, 131, 135, 143, 145, 147, 179, 185, 195, 197, 199, 201, 203-205, 209, 227, 230, 235, 241, 246
Bobrow/Thomas & Associates 212
Bohemian Club 58
Booth Computing Center 179, 227
Brackenridge, Marian 257
Bradbury, Louis 26, 28
Braun Athletic Center 236-237, 239
Braun, Carl F 211-212, 239, 251
Bridge Laboratory of Physics 42-46, 51, 53, 57, 61-63, 115, 195, 219, 257
Bridge, Dr. Norman 25, 42
Bridges, Dan 239
Broad Center for the Biological Sciences 262-263
Broad, Eli 261-263
Brown, Harold 58, 201, 209
Brunner, Michael C. 235
Building and Grounds Committee 162, 180
Burke, Walter 241
Buwalda, John P. 115, 118
byzantine 35, 73
Calder, A. Stirling 25-26, 28, 116, 204-205, 212-213, 255

California Institute Associates 94
California Native Garden 166
Caltech Associates 76, 128, 227
Caltech Submillimeter Observatory 104
Frost, Camilla Chandler 261
Campbell Laboratory 177
Campbell, Jim 228
Campus Planning Committee 201
Carver Mead 228
Casanova, Aldo 257
central library 10, 46, 61, 162, 177, 193-195, 197, 199
Central Plant Cooling Towers and Cogeneration 239, 241
Chandler Dining Hall 246
Chandler, Harry 145-146, 180, 246-247
Chapel of the Intercession 62
Charles C. Lauritsen Laboratory of High Energy Physics 181
Charles Luckman Associates 173, 195
Chemical Engineering Laboratory 71, 211, 219, 241-242
Christy, Robert F. 209
Church Laboratory of Chemical Biology 166, 175, 177
Church, Norman W. 166, 174-175, 177, 212-213
Churriguera 35, 40
Churrigueresque 35, 40, 44, 63, 76, 88, 108, 111, 121, 193, 223-224
City Planning Commission 188
Clark, Alson 31
Clark, Donald S. 143
Clements, Stiles O. 174-175
Cleveland Wrecking Company 249
Coate, Roland E. 128, 135-136
coelostat telescope 104
coffee shop 177, 180
Colonel Seeley Wintersmith Mudd 116, 195, 197
Compton effect 43
Council, Lucile 162-163
Court of Honour 39
Court of Man 202
Cram, Goodhue & Ferguson 32
Crellin, Edward and Amy 76-77, 112, 116, 212-213
Culbertson, James A. 53, 55
Culbertson Hall 9, 53, 55, 57-58, 90, 177, 185-186
Dabney Garden 84, 160, 204-205, 242, 252, 257
Dabney Hall of the Humanities 63, 83-84, 86-90, 146, 160, 203, 242, 255
Dabney House 153-155
Dabney, Joseph B. 146-147
Daugherty, Robert, 140
Department of Geology 115
Devil's Gate Dam 252
diaper pattern 47, 51, 90, 178
Dixon, John Morris 174
dormitories 9, 128-129, 131, 143, 145-147, 150, 153, 155, 163, 166, 168, 173, 177, 180, 182, 224, 230-231, 233, 246, 255
Douglas World Cruiser 81
Downs-Lauritsen Physics Building 97, 179, 227

Downs, George W. 181
Dreyfuss, Henry 203
DuBridge, Lee Alvin 171-175, 177, 185, 188, 190, 193-195, 197, 201, 203, 236
Dunn, Gano 67
Durfee Foundation 230
Dynasty 257
Eagleson, Harvey 257
Earhart Plant Research facility 177
East Bridge 43-44, 51, 53, 57, 63, 219
Edison High Tension Laboratory 51
Edward Durrell Stone 185, 188
Einstein, Albert 138-140
Engelmann oak 90, 159
Engineering and Science, 51, 79 150
Epstein, Paul 139
Eton College 143
Etrog, Sorel 257
Everhart, Thomas E. 13, 217
Executive Council 42, 61, 67, 116, 131, 140, 171
Fagan, Peter 257
Faience tile 44-45
Fairchild Library of Engineering 71, 241-242, 245
Fairchild, Sherman 241-242
Farrand, Beatrix 157, 160, 162-163, 249, 252
Farrand, Max 160
Feynman, Richard 155
fiddler crab 114
Fire, Water, Earth and Air 43, 124
Firestone Flight Sciences 179, 181
Firestone Tire & Rubber Company 181
Fleming House 153, 225
Fleming, Arthur 23, 25, 35, 39, 46, 53, 68, 71, 73, 75, 107-108, 111, 129, 136, 139, 147, 153, 157, 160, 171
Flewelling & Moody 197-198
Florentine 139
Fort, Robert 212
Foucault Pendulum 199
Fowler, Kate 53, 58
Fox, Lucia 162
Franklin Thomas Laboratory of Engineering 173
Freed, James 14, 262
GALCIT 80-81
Gates Annex 73-74, 162
Gates Chemistry Laboratory 39-40, 42, 57, 63, 86, 90, 175, 203-204, 209, 212
Gates, Charles 39-40, 73-74, 76
Gates, Peter 39-40, 73-74
Gebhard, David 197
Geochemistry 172
George W. Downs Laboratory of Physics 179, 181, 227
Giovannini, Joseph 150
Glee Club 190
Goldberger, Marvin 10, 209
Goodhue Associates 9, 65, 68, 71-72, 76, 79-80, 86, 90, 94-96, 108, 111, 116, 121, 131, 147, 162, 185-186, 228, 241
Goodhue, Bertram Grosvenor 9, 29, 31-37, 39-51, 53-56, 58-59, 61-65, 67-68, 71-76, 79, 84, 88, 107, 111-114, 116, 127,

129, 131, 135-136, 143, 146-147, 150, 157, 166, 168-169, 171, 173-175, 177-179, 185-186, 193, 197, 199, 207, 212, 219-220, 223-225, 227-229, 232, 242-243, 252, 255, 265

Goodstein, Judith 67, 171-172

Gothic 35, 53, 62, 113

Graduate School of Aeronautics 9, 67, 79-81, 97

Great Depression 116

Greco-Roman 132, 139

Green Hotel 18, 25

Greene, Henry 143-144

Greenstein, Jesse 172

Grey, Elmer 23-25, 28, 31, 34-35, 39-40, 53-54, 143-144, 204, 212, 239

Griswold Conservation Associates 239

Gropius, Walter 174

Guggenheim Aeronautics Laboratory 79-81, 97, 173, 177, 179, 252

Guggenheim, Daniel 79

Hale, George Ellery 13, 21-23, 25, 31, 35, 39-40, 42, 46, 53, 61, 64, 67-69, 71, 73, 76, 83, 88, 90, 93, 95-96, 104, 107, 111, 115-117, 127-129, 131, 139-140, 147, 166, 171, 212, 255, 257, 265

Hale, Margaret 257

Hall of the Associates 135, 137, 139

Hamrol, Lloyd 259

Hellmuth, Obata & Kassabaum 209

High Potential Research Laboratory 44

High Volts 46-48, 51, 63, 175, 195

Holmes & Narver 179

Hood, John H. 150, 246

Housner, George 203

Hunt & Grey 23-25, 28, 31, 34-35, 39, 143-144, 204

Hunt, George S. 88

Hunt, Myron 23-25, 28, 31, 34-35, 37, 39, 88, 107, 143-144, 162

Hunt's Heartache 25, 37

Huntington Library 127, 139, 160

Hydrodynamic Laboratory 173

Institute Archives 128, 138, 197

International Education Board 93

International Style 174, 193

Iser, Gustav 95

Italian cypresses 157

Italian Renaissance 136, 139

James Irvine Foundation 212

James R. Killian 185

Jefferson, Thomas 24

Jenkins, Grant V. 143

Jennings, Paul 203

Jensen, Holger & Helen Webster 255

Jet Propulsion Laboratory (JPL) 80, 252

Johnson, Reginald 128, 131, 135-136

Jones, A. Quincy 249

Karman Laboratory of Fluid Mechanics & Jet Propulsion 179

Kaufmann, Gordon B. 9, 125, 128, 130-132, 135-136, 138-140, 144, 146-150, 152, 154-155, 162-164, 168, 173, 180, 182, 193-195, 220, 223-224, 231-232, 236, 242, 246, 255, 265

Keck Engineering Laboratory 179-180

Kellogg Radiation Laboratory 195

Kerckhoff Biology 177

Kerckhoff I: 108-110, 113, 116, 117, 121, 177-178

Kerckhoff, William G. 108-111, 128

Kerckhoff II: 110, 112, 114, 116

Knudsen, Vern O. 188

Konishi, Mark 228

Kurt Meyer Partners 217

Kwabena Boahen 228

lambrequin 40, 44, 122, 224

Land Images 160, 206, 251-252

Landry, Gerald 81

Last Supper, The 155

Lauritsen, Charles C. 181

Lawrie, Lee 48, 61-62

Le Corbusier 174

Lehman, Robert 145

Lehman, Tom 239

Leland, Malcolm 198-199

Lloyd-Smith, Marjorie Fleming 53

Lockett, Thomas A. 252

loggia 88, 90, 131, 136, 139, 149-150, 153

Los Angeles 2, 17, 23, 25, 61, 128, 132, 135, 146, 163, 173-174, 197, 201, 203, 223, 255, 257

Luckman, Charles 173-174, 177, 179, 183, 185, 187, 194-195, 197, 201-202, 236

Lunar 257

machine shop 21-22, 79, 94, 96-97, 100

Mammary Hall 179

Martin, Albert C. 223, 246-247

Marsh, Smith & Powell 236

Marston, Sylvanus 143

Mashrabiyya 44

master plan 9-10, 23, 29, 31, 33, 35, 37, 39, 41, 47, 49, 53, 59, 62-63, 68, 88, 107, 111, 166, 168-169, 173-174, 177, 197, 201, 215, 217-220, 223-224, 226, 228-230, 232, 236-239, 241-246, 252, 254, 256, 258-259, 262, 264-266, 268-270

Master Plan Report 1971 201

Mayan 47, 63, 75, 90, 179

Mayers, Francis L. S. 68

Mayers, Murray and Phillip 68, 171

mechanical engineering 173, 211

Mediterranean 24-25, 128, 136, 140, 163, 180, 182, 207

Memorial Building 33-34, 37, 40, 42-44, 63, 73, 77, 88, 107, 111, 121, 157, 166, 168, 177, 193, 197

Memorial Fountain 62

Meyer & Allen Associates 217

Michelson, Albert 140

Michizane, Sugawara 257

Mies Van Der Rohe, Ludwig 174

Millikan Pond 257

Millikan, Clark Blanchard 80

Millikan, Robert Andrew 13, 40, 42, 44, 46, 51, 61, 67-69, 77, 79, 83, 107, 113, 121, 140, 143, 145-146, 160, 162, 171-172, 174, 195-199, 203, 235, 241, 251-252, 255, 257

Millikan's School 67, 171-172

MIT 21, 23, 39-40, 95, 145, 171, 185, 261

modern movement 174
modernism 174, 199
Moore Laboratory of Engineering 226-228
Moore Ruble Yudell 230, 241
Moore, Charles 230
Moore, Gordon & Betty 226, 259
Moorish 35, 47, 88, 109, 163, 177, 179
Morgan, Thomas Hunt 93, 107-108, 111, 113-114, 171, 247
Morris, William 32
Morristoe Astroscience Laboratory 239
Mudd, Harvey S. 118, 195
Mudd, Seeley G. 121-122, 193, 195-199, 207
Mudd, Seeley W. 115-116, 121-122, 195
Munro, William B. 83, 139, 145, 162
Muntz, Jan Furey 136, 139-140
Murray, Oscar 68, 171
music auditorium 53-55
National Academy of Sciences 21, 61, 67, 185
National Cancer Institute 211
National Science Foundation 181
Nebraska 61, 199
Neff, Wallace 128, 136
Neher, H.V. 199
Neptune Thomas Davis 227
Neptune, Thomas & Associates 179, 227
Neutra, Richard J. 201
New York City 32, 61-62
Newberry 22, 25
Nobel Prize 67, 76, 107, 261
Norman W. Church Laboratory 166, 175, 177
North Mudd 115-116, 121-122, 124, 196, 202
Noyes, Arthur Amos 13, 39-40, 42, 67, 69, 73, 75-76, 83, 90, 107, 135, 145, 171, 180, 182, 259
nuclear physics 97
O.K. Earl Corporation 239
O'Keefe, Tony 227
O'Melveny, Henry 128
Obata, Gyo 209
Observatory Council 93
Olive Walk 165, 180, 225, 252
Oliver, Richard 31
optical shop 94, 96-97, 99
Oud, J.J.P 174
Owens Valley Radio Observatory 104
Paddock Field 236
Paddock, Charlie 236
Paleontology Museum 117, 119, 121
Palomar Observatory 93, 95-96, 104, 257
Panama-California Exposition 31, 73
Panel of the Nine Muses 58
Parsons-Gates Hall of Administration 212
Pasadena Beautiful Award 190
Pasadena Civic Auditorium 185
Pasadena Music & Art Association 53
Pauling, Linus 75-76, 172, 174
Payne, Theodore 166
Pei Cobb Freed & Partners 14, 262
Pereira & Luckman 173-174, 177, 179, 185, 187, 194-195, 197, 236

Pereira, William 173-174, 177, 179, 181, 194-195
Performing Arts Series 190
Phillip, Hardie 68, 71, 73, 107, 116
Physical Plant 168, 173, 177, 212
Piccirilli 40
planetary science 207, 219
plateresque, 35, 110, 122
portales 35, 37, 40, 90, 150, 193, 223, 232, 265
Portanova, Joseph 255
Porte-cochère 131,136
Porter, Russell 93-97, 100
Porter's Arch 96
Progressive Architecture 174
Provost 172, 209
Prufrock House 211
Pueblo architecture 63, 83, 88
Radiation Therapy 196
Radio Club 247
Ralph M. Parsons Foundation 212
Ramo Auditorium 257
Red Door Cafe 247
Reynolds, George W. 140
Ricketts, Louis D., Dr. & Mrs. 147
Ricketts House 150, 153, 204-205
Risley, Gould & Van Heuklyn 180
Robinson Astrophysics 76, 97, 99-100, 102-104
Robinson, Henry W. 46, 93, 116, 162, 171
Rockefeller Foundation 93
Rose Bowl 235
Rosen, Benjamin M. 261
Rosenstone, Robert 239
Royal Tyson 203
Russell, George Vernon 207
San Diego 31, 73, 75, 230
San Francisco 58, 227, 262
San Gabriel mountains 188, 252
San Juan Capistrano 40
San Pasqual Pathway 219, 250-252
San Rafael 116
Sargent, Charles Sprague 157, 160
Saturn 104
Scherer, James A. B. 21-23, 25, 35, 37, 39, 53, 67, 157, 159
Scherer, Paul A. 257
Scherer-Hale Memorial Fund 257
Schneider, Edwin H. 257
Schoeller, Phillip 145
Scholtz, Walter 145
Science for Mankind 202, 206
Science Museum 33, 42, 225
Scott Brown Gymnasium 187, 239
Scott Brown Trust 236
sculpture 26, 48, 51, 81, 178, 255, 257, 259
Searing, Helen 113
Seeley G. Mudd Building of Geophysics & Planetary
Seismological Research Laboratory 116
Sharp, Robert 172
Sherman Fairchild Foundation 241
Sherman Fairchild Library of Engineering & Applied Science 241-242

Silver, Leon 252, 255
Sloan Mathematics & Physics 178, 202
Smaus, Robert 163
Smeraldi, Giovanni Battista 132, 139
Smith, Mrs. Dan Throop 252
Smith, David 257
Smith, Hallett 172
Smith, Powell & Morgridge 180
SMP-SHG 262
South Mudd 207
Southern California Edison Co. 23, 46, 51
Spalding Engineering Laboratory 241
Spanish Colonial 62, 68, 136
spectrograph 99-100
Agnew, Spiro 205
Stanton, J.E.193
steam plant 71, 73, 241-242
Steele Laboratory 202
Stein, Clarence 73, 75, 86, 90, 108, 131
Steinmetz, David 257
Stewart, Albert 113, 247
Stiny, George 174
Student Union 143, 147, 236
Superior Oil Company 179
Sylmar Earthquake 71, 203, 212
synchrotron 97
Taj Mahal 37
Tau Beta Pi 257
Tenjin 257
The Dugout 143-144
Thomas J. Watson, Sr. Laboratories of Applied
Physics 209-210, 223, 252
Thomas, Franklin 173
Thomas, S. Seymour 23, 69
Throop, Amos Gager 17-18, 31, 265
Throop Club 144, 168, 236, 247
Throop Gardens 249
Tolman-Bacher house 220
Tooby, George 257
Tournament of Roses 57, 235
Tournament Park 220, 235-236
Treasure Room 87-88, 90, 136
trilobite 121, 122
Tympanums 150, 227
University of Chicago 42, 190, 209
University of Virginia 24
Van de Graaff accelerator 179
Van Pelt, Garrett 131, 143
Vatican 26, 28, 132, 239
Von Kármán, Theodore 79-80
Vreeland, Tim 223, 225
W.M. Keck Observatory 104
W.M. Keck Foundation 179, 252
Washington, D.C. 61, 160, 201, 262
Watson, Earnest C. 42, 44, 180
Watson, Floyd R. 190
Watson, Thomas J. Sr. 209-210
Ways & Means Committee 195

West Bridge 43, 45-46, 62-63, 115
West Court 55, 88, 107, 111, 116-117, 163, 197, 199, 228, 252, 265
West Millikan Mall 252
West Patio 131, 136, 140, 166, 255
Whittier Narrows 80
Wilson, James Perry 84, 115-116, 178, 186
wind tunnel 79-80
Winnett Student Center 144, 246
Winnett, P.G. 138, 180, 246-247
Winter, Robert 23, 197
World War I: 35, 42, 67
World War II: 79-80, 96, 171, 174, 201
Wright Brothers 79
Wright, Frank Lloyd 174, 179
Wrought-iron 44, 90, 139, 150, 160, 231
Yoch, Florence 162-163, 165-166
Yoch, James J. 162-163
Yudell, Buzz 230-231, 241

Text set in Monotype Dante

Initial capitals used at the beginning of each
chapter are set in Cheltenham, designed by
Bertram Goodhue.